Welcome to Balaton

1

Lake Balaton, Badacsony Hill in the background
© OliverLeicher/iStock

Getting to Budapest and Lake Balaton

FROM FERENC LISZT AIRPORT

Budapest's international airport is 22km/13mi southeast of the city centre. Both regular and low cost airlines fly into Terminal 2 (the only terminal in service). www.bud.hu/en

Bus

Bus **100E** goes direct to Deák Ferenc tér, a square in the centre of Budapest *(1 hr journey)*, also a key transport hub. Buses operate between 5am and 1.20am, every 20min. Ft900 *(from the BKK kiosk in Terminal 2 arrivals hall)*.

Airport minibus/Shuttle

The minibus will drop you wherever you want in the city. Operates 24hrs, every 30min. Book ahead online *([1] 550 0000, minibud.hu/en)* or buy tickets in the arrivals hall in euros or forints: €19.50/approx Ft6,500 for one passenger; €10.60/approx. Ft3,500 per person for two, etc.

Taxi

From the taxi rank at the arrivals hall. Around Ft7, 200 to the city centre.

TO LAKE BALATON

By car

Collect your car from the airport. The rental companies are in the arrivals hall *(follow signs, see p. 94).*

Tihany village and the Benedictine Abbey
© Laszlo Szirtesi/Shutterstock

Metro, bus and tram
Info: bkk.hu
Hours: 4.30am–11.50pm+night service
Tariff: Ft350 (Ft450 on the bus, with the exact change). 10 tickets – Ft3,000.
Transfer ticket: Valid to transfer between types of transport (e.g. bus to tram) Ft530 (1 transfer single journey)
Useful passes:
3 day travel card – Valid for the whole Budapest transport network, including night services: Ft4,150.
Budapest Kártya (Budapest Card) – Valid for the whole Budapest transport network and free or reduced price entry in many museums. Ft6,490 for 24hrs, Ft9,990/48hrs and Ft12,990/72hrs.

Lake Balaton is around 75min from the airport via the M7 motorway. At Balatonvilágos, head towards Balatonfüred for the north shore or towards Siófok for the south shore.

By train

From Déli Station in Budapest (terminus of the metro line M2), there's around one direct train per hour to Balatonfüred *(2hrs journey, approx. Ft2,800)* and to Siófok *(1hr 20min journey, approx. Ft2,300)*. Book ahead at: mavcsoport.hu/en

By bus

Book ahead at: volanbusz.hu/en

Unmissable
Our picks for must-see sights:

Szent-György Hill ★★★
(Balaton) Map BC5–6,
 p. 44

Hévíz thermal lake★★★
(Balaton) Map A6, p. 48

Veszprém★ (Balaton)
Map E3, p. 53

Parliament Building★★★
(Budapest)
Map C3, p. 20

Székesfehérvár★★
(Balaton)
Map GH2, p. 58

4

North shore★★ (Balaton)
Map A6–E3, ♿ p. 28

Keszthely★★ (Balaton)
Map A6, ♿ p. 50

Thermal baths★★
(Budapest) Map D7
and G1, ♿ p. 18 and 24

5

Tihany★★★ (Balaton)
Map E5, ♿ p. 38

**Buda Castle and the Castle
District★★★** (Budapest)
Map C5, ♿ p. 16

Our top picks

BUDAPEST

💜 **Admire the panoramic view of the Danube** from the terrace of Buda Castle. Or even higher up, from the dome of the magnificent Hungarian National Gallery, which occupies a wing of the castle (p. 17).

💜 **Rub shoulders with young hipsters in a 'ruin bar'** *(romkocsma)* in Erzsébetváros, the Old Jewish Quarter, where the delapidated buildings abandoned during the Communist era have been transformed into bars for party people and night owls (p. 21 & 84).

💜 **Do the rounds of the Secessionist buildings** and discover their amazing interiors. Special mention must go to the Museum of Applied Arts (p. 25), along with the vast array of Secessionst objects and furniture at the House of Hungarian Art Nouveau (p. 20).

LAKE BALATON

💜 **Escape to the country** at Szántódpuszta Tourist and Cultural Centre, an open-air museum where you can see animals and 18C and 19C farm buildings, or enjoy a ride in a horse-drawn carriage (p. 32).

💜 **Celebrate the Hungarian water buffalo** in the Kápolnapuszta Reserve, where you can see one of Hungary's rare herds (p. 33).

💜 **Taste the mineral water from the Lajos Kossuth drinking fountain** in Balatonfüred, Lake Balaton's elegant spa resort with a touch of Old Europe glamour and nostalgia (p. 37).

💜 **Wander through the lovely shaded streets of Sümeg,** a pretty town crowned by one of Hungary's most beautiful castles (p. 45).

💜 **Discover Hungary's royal roots** at the National Memorial site in Székesfehérvár, where the country's first king, Stephen I, rests alongside twenty other monarchs (p. 58).

© Botond Horvath/Shutterstock

Öskü Chapel

© ivabalk/Pixabay

Water sports on Lake Balaton

♥ **Enjoy the shallow waters of Lake Balaton** to try out or perfect your windsurfing and sailing techniques. Children can enjoy splashing about in the warm, shallow water, too (p. 26).

♥ **Enjoy the sound of your own voice again and again** on Echo Hill on Tihany Peninsula, where an echo has been known to repeat as many as 16 times (p. 40).

♥ **Discover the small wine-growing region of Somló**. After having been neglected during the Communist regime, since the 1980s it has enjoyed a new lease of life with new vines planted (p. 46).

♥ **Try a very slightly radioactive mud bath** in Héviz: the mud covers the bottom of the thermal lake and is said to have curative properties when applied to the skin (p. 49).

♥ **Go round in circles in the unusual round Catholic church** in the small village of Öskü near Veszprém. Looking a little like a mushroom, it dates back to the 11/12C (p. 57).

♥ **Try some spelunking by boat across the clear water in the caves** under the pretty town of Tapolca. The mineral-enriched and dust-free air underground is helpful for respiratory problems (p. 46).

Budapest and Lake Balaton in 6 days

DAY 1

▶ Morning

From the **Chain Bridge★★** (p. 18), take the funicular up to **Buda Castle★★★** (p. 16) from where you can enjoy a spectacular view before visiting one of the castle's two museums: the **Hungarian National Gallery★★** or **Budapest History Museum★** (p. 17).

▶ Afternoon

Take lunch in the **Castle District★★★** then stroll through its lanes, stopping off to look around the lovely **Matthias Church★★** (p. 18).

▶ Evening

Cross the river via the famous Chain Bridge, then dine in one of the restaurants on the **Danube Promenade★★** (p. 18), with its beautiful panoramic views back across to Buda lit up at night.

DAY 2

▶ Morning

Discover the historic centre of Pest, starting in **Lipótváros★★★** (p. 20), where you can visit the **Parliament Building★★★** (p. 20), a city icon. Stroll through this attractive district and visit the **House of Hungarian Art Nouveau★** (p. 20).

▶ Afternoon

Have lunch in one of the many restaurants in **Belváros★★** (p. 21), the other beating heart of the town's historic centre. Make the most of the shops in **Váci utca** and pop into **Dohány Street Synagogue★★** (p. 22), but don't linger too long in winter as it closes at 4pm.

▶ Evening

As the afternoon draws to a close, head for the Old Jewish Quarter, **Erzsébetváros★** (p. 21), and wander its streets to soak up the atmosphere – it's a popular haunt

8

© Bertrand Gardel/hemis.fr

Boat trip on Lake Balaton

for partygoers. Dine in one of the district's hip restaurants before ending your evening in a *romkocsma* (ruin bar).

DAY 3

▶ *Morning*

Walk up **Andrássy Avenue**★★ *(p. 22)*. one of Budapest's grand boulevards. Depending on your interests, visit the **State Opera House**★★, the **Franz Liszt Museum**★ or the **House of Terror**★★ *(p. 22)*, which are all in the same area.

▶ *Afternoon*

Take the metro to **Heroes' Square** and the **Museum of Fine Arts** ★★★ *(p. 24)*, which houses remarkable collections of paintings by the European masters. Next, make your way to **Széchenyi Baths**★★★ *(p. 24)*, in a setting that simply could not be more Baroque.

▶ *Evening*

Dine in the area around **St. Stephen's Basilica**★★ *(p. 21)*, especially lively at this time with its many bars and restaurants.

DAY 4

▶ *Morning*

Head to **Balatonfüred**★ *(p. 34)*, one of Lake Balaton's key resorts, by train or car. You might stop off to enjoy a tasty lunch in one of the bistros in the nearby wine-growing villages.

▶ *Afternoon*

Enjoy the nostalgic atmosphere in Balatonfüred with a stroll by the lake and a visit to the small local museums.

Sample its curative waters before a swim in the lake.

▶ *Evening*

Make your way to Tihany for dinner and an overnight stay.

DAY 5

▶ *Morning*

Discover **Tihany** ★★★ *(p. 38)*, its village, abbey and paths. Enjoy lunch in one of its restaurants with views.

▶ *Afternoon*

Take a stroll among the lavender on Tihany Peninsula or the vines in **Badacsony**★★★ *(p. 44)*, or opt for the beach instead/as well. Sip some wine in a bar perched high on the slopes.

▶ *Evening*

You're in luck! Badacsony has many good restaurants so take advantage.

DAY 6

▶ *Morning*

Head to the small, pretty town of **Keszthely**★★ *(p. 50)* and Festetics Palace, one of Hungary's best preserved castles. Stroll through the town and have a spot of lunch.

▶ *Afternoon*

Stop at **Hévíz thermal lake**★★★ *(p. 48)* for a little relaxation and wellbeing in a stunning location. ▶

▶ *Evening*

Choose between a local tavern or a gastronomic restaurant. On your way to Budapest, stop off in a resort on the lake's south shore *(p. 30)* for a last Hungarian gourmet experience.

Budapest and Lake Balaton in 8 days

DAYS 1 TO 5

See the suggested tour p. 8–9.

DAY 6

▶ Morning

On your way to Keszthely, stop at Szigliget and climb up to **Szigliget Castle★** (p. 29) for a glimpse of medieval history and unforgettable views of Lake Balaton. Enjoy lunch in a village tavern.

▶ Afternoon

In **Keszthely★★** (p. 50), visit Festetics Palace, one of the best-preserved in Hungary, not forgetting its estate and museums. Explore the lanes of this pretty town before making your way to one of its popular beaches.

▶ Evening

Enjoy a stroll by the lake before a spot of dinner.

DAY 7

▶ Morning

Head to **Hévíz thermal lake★★★** (p. 48), for a couple of hours of relaxation and pampering in a beautiful location. Waterlilies flower on the lake beneath the spa pavilions mounted on stilts and in winter steam rises from the water in an ethereal and atmospheric mist.

Have lunch at Hévíz or enjoy a picnic on **Kányavári Island★** (p. 33), in the **Kis-Balaton★** (Little Balaton, p. 33).

▶ Afternoon

On Lake Balaton's south shore, stop at Sphere Lookout at **Balatonboglár★** (p. 30) for some fantastic views of the lake. Finish your afternoon at the **Szántódpuszta Tourist and Cultural Centre★** (p. 32), a wooded park that is also an open-air museum, where you can see exhibits and displays about the traditional rural way of life.

▶ Evening

Try one of the many local taverns or gourmet restaurants in the area.

DAY 8

▶ Morning

On your way back to Budapest, stop in **Székesfehérvár★★** (p. 58), with its well-preserved Baroque centre. Visit the **National Memorial★** where thirty-seven Hungarian kings were crowned and twenty are buried, including Stephen I, founder of the Hungarian kingdom in the year 1000.

▶ Afternoon

Wander Székesfehérvár's lanes lined with historic churches and museums.

▶ Evening

Have dinner here, too, before making your way back to Budapest.

10

Vineyards in the Lake Balaton region

Discovering
Lake Balaton

13

Pier on Lake Balaton, Keszthely
© Jon Arnold Images/hemis.fr

Lake Balaton today

Have you thought about extending your stay in Hungary? It is the inevitable question after a few days in **Budapest**. And fortunately, nothing could be simpler since Lake Balaton, one of the stars of the Hungarian tourist industry, is just two hours away by rail or road. After all, most visitors to Hungary arrive first in its capital – a city that reflects a country with a thousand different faces and a wealth of riches. Many visitors spend a few days in Budapest, exploring its beguiling combination of Eastern and Western influences, falling under the spell of its glorious Secessionst architecture, Viennese-style cafés and inviting Turkish baths. But then it's time to venture a little further afield to enjoy the best of both worlds, city and the regions, and head to the sunlit shores of **Lake Balaton**.

The lake can be found in the western half of the country, stretched out in the sun rather like a long, thin chilli pepper (appropriately enough!) 77km/47 miles long, between the elegant town of Keszthely at the western tip of the north shore and the busy seaside resorts, such as Balatonfüred, towards its north-eastern end.

This beautiful lake is like a vast oasis among the green and wooded hills of Transdanubia. As one of the largest lakes in Europe, it is almost on the scale of an inland sea, with shimmering water that changes colour with the weather, from all shades of blue to a deep turquoise and even jade green, the kind of colours that seem unreal at these latitudes. And in the distance, dozens of small white dots – the sails of the many yachts that criss-cross the lake under a brilliant blue sky – complete the picture. Amateur sailors are in their element here.

A world of water

The lake does not represent the only presence of water in the area, there are more hidden and secretive waters here in the form of the thermal springs that emerge from deep underground. The Balaton region has been known for its spa treatments and cures since the early 19C, when **Balatonfüred**, its oldest resort, attracted the Austro-Hungarian aristocracy. They were fond of taking alkaline water cures and Balaton mud baths – interspersed with swimming in the lake, of course. As elsewhere in Europe, the presence of high society for several months at a time attracted many others, including artists, lured away from the pleasures of Budapest, its theatres and concerts, who came to take advantage of the light here. Lake Balaton began to take on a glittering reputation, launching it as the place to see and be seen, which continues to this day.

The spirit of Belle Epoque Europe still lingers in the centre of Balatonfüred, with its charming period villas. Elsewhere, other chapters from

Hungarian history have left their mark, too, from the challenging lives of the peasants in their thatched cottages, as can be seen at the **Szántód** open-air museum, to the Communist era holiday complexes, traces of which still linger on the southern shores of the lake.

Close by, just a little further west, is one of the stars of Hungary's show, the beautiful thermal lake at **Hévíz**. People come here to float in its warm waters amid water lilies, but when the air cools and the first frosts arrive, mist drifts over the lake in an enchanting fashion.

Just as amazing is the lake at nearby **Tapolca**, slightly north of Lake Balaton. Two subterranean springs have carved out a cave system beneath the town, part of which can be explored by boat on a magical trip on the clear water in this extraordinary network of caverns.

A beautiful hinterland

If the Lake Balaton region has long relied on its seaside resorts and thermal springs to draw in visitors, it has plenty of other attractions, such as its wine-growing villages and vineyards. On the slopes of the **Badacsony** massif, where some of the best Hungarian wines are produced, you can taste wine on open-air terraces, surrounded by the vines that made them. Tapolca enjoys a spectacular setting surrounded by cone-shaped wooded hills, which are in fact ancient volcanoes. And wherever you go, you are never far from a stunning view from one of the many observation towers.

© Philippe Body/hemis.fr

15

Sunbathing on the pier

There are small historic towns to explore with their castles and palaces. From **Székesfehérvár** with its beautiful Baroque architecture, churches and museums, to **Veszprém**, where the queens of Hungary came to be crowned. Add to these **Kis-Balaton** (Little Balaton), a paradise for ecologists and nature lovers and not far away, the charming town of **Keszthely** with its well-preserved palace. So there's no time to lose, Lake Balaton here we come!

The best of Budapest★★★

Bordering the banks of the majestic River Danube, the city is divided into two distinct entities with their own individual characters: Buda on the right (west) bank and Pest on the left (east) bank. To the west, you'll find the hills of Buda with its imposing castle in a spectacular location, the first stop on any visit to the city. The breathtaking view from this lofty vantage point makes it easy to understand why the Danube panorama is included in the Unesco World Heritage List. To the east, the Pest area undoubtedly represents the pinnacle of the mighty Austro-Hungarian Empire.

Hungary's capital city has so much to offer that you could quite easily while away many a day here. But for those on a brief visit, (re)discovering Budapest as the gateway to Hungary, we have selected the best of the best for you, for a three-day lightning tour of this marvellous and exciting city.

▶**Info: Tourinform Office – Sütő utca** – *Sütő utca 2 (Belváros, near Deák Ferenc tér), open 8am–8pm;* **Tourinform Office – Budapest Airport** – *Terminal 2A, open 8am–10pm; Terminal 2B, open 10am–10pm.* **Call center** – *℘ (1) 438 8080. Open 7am–7pm (in English).* **Mobile information booths** are dotted around Budapest's tourist areas during the holiday season *(open 9am–6pm).*

▶**Tip:** The Budapest Card gives you access to numerous places of interest free or with a discount, as well as free travel on public transport. (👣*See p. 96).*

Detachable map, Budapest.
👣 *See Addresses pp. 66, 74, 80, 82, 86 and 88.*

VÁRNEGYED★★★

(Buda Castle District)
BC4–5 *Access: bus 16, 16A, 105 Clark Ádám tér, or* 🚋 *19, 41 Clark Ádám tér. Then climb the steps, or take the funicular or Budapest Castle Bus (5 stops in the Castle District, operates 9am–4pm, Ft2,400 or free with the Budapest Card).*
The fact that this is a Unesco World Heritage Site says it all. The castle and royal palace complex is in a superb location on top of a hill and hosts several world-class museums. Nearby, beautiful Renaissance and Baroque buildings jostle for position in the Old Town. And as a bonus, the views down over the Hungarian capital and the Danube are simply stunning.

Sikló (Funicular)
Open 7.30am–10pm. Ft1,400, round trip Ft2,000. Board the funicular from near the Chain Bridge. Its wooden cars have been ferrying people up to the castle since 1870.

The Castle

C5 Budai vár★★★ (Buda Castle) – This immense castle and royal palace originally dates from the 13C but was extensively remodelled under the Habsburgs and then rebuilt after the Second World War. Its very imposing Baroque facade looks down onto the Danube in dramatic fashion, more than 300m/984ft below.

As you enter the castle through the ornate neo-Baroque stone gateway with iron railings, look for the bronze sculpture of a bird high up on a pillar to the left. With a sword between its claws and its wings stretched out against the blue sky, it is as if it is about to take flight. This is the mythological **turul** bird, the emblem of the Magyar tribes.

The **view★★** from the castle precinct is amazing and makes an excellent introduction to the city with, from left to right, Margaret Island, the Parliament Building, the Chain Bridge, St. Stephen's Basilica, Elisabeth Bridge, Liberty Bridge and, in the distance, Gellért Hill, the citadel and the Liberty Statue. The whole of Budapest unfolds before you at your feet.

Magyar Nemzeti Galéria★★ (Hungarian National Gallery) – *Szent György tér. ☎ (1) 201 9082. mng.hu. Open Tue–Sun, 10am–6pm. Ft3,200. Audioguide in English Ft800.*

The gallery covers Hungarian pictorial and sculptural art from the Middle Ages to the 20C. In the splendid setting of the former throne room you can see a fine collection of late Gothic altarpieces – triptychs and polyptychs from the 15C and early 16C. Among the 19C artists featured in the gallery are Mihály Munkácsy and László Paál. You can also see works based on epic scenes from history, such as *The Baptism of Vajk* by Gyula Benczúr and Miklós Zrínyi and the *Siege of Szigetvár* by Johann Peter Krafft.

☺ If the weather is clear climb up to the **dome**, from where there is a stunning **view★★** of the city *(access from the 3rd floor, open 10am–5pm, Ft1,000).*

☺ The National Gallery is due to move in 2021 to the museum hub in Városliget (City Park).

Budapesti Történeti Múzeum★ (Budapest History Museum) – *Szent György ter 2. ☎ (1) 487 8800. www.btm.hu. Open Tue–Sun, Mar–Oct, 10am–6pm; Nov–Feb, 10am–4pm. Ft2,000.* The museum explores Budapest's history via various rooms, collections and artefacts: carved stonework from archeological sites, jewellery, ceramics and so on. One hall displays some beautifully expressive Gothic statues. Rooms with vaulted ceilings, many dating from the late 14C/early 15C, were discovered during building work and hark back to the castle's pre-Habsburg incarnation (lower floors and basements), along with a royal chapel from the 14C French Angevin kings who reigned 1309–82.

Old town★★★

B4 It's true you will see plenty of tourists wandering the Old Town, but seeing the beautiful buildings that line the streets (*utca* in Hungarian), it's no wonder. Our favourites are: **Úri utca**★★ (the longest), **Táncsics Mihály utca**★★ (Baroque and neo-classical buildings with colourful facades) and **Tárnok utca** (more painted facades, decorated with Baroque corbels and other architectural elements).

Mátyás templom★★ (Matthias Church) – *Szentháromság tér. ℘ (1) 488 7716. matyas-templom.hu. Open Mon–Fri, 9am–5pm; Sat, 9am–2.30pm, Sun 1pm–5pm. Ft1,800.* With the delicate stonework of its bell tower and its colourful roof of glazed tiles, the church is one of the most visited sites in Budapest. The oldest parts date back to the 13C, but the church has been greatly modified since then, notably in the 15C by Matthias (Mátyás) Corvinus, after whom it is named, and again during the 19C and the reign of Emperor Franz Joseph and Empress Elisabeth, who were crowned king and queen of Hungary here in 1867. Rebuilt after the Second World War, the building has now regained its former glory. The interior is painted with geometric and vegetal motifs in a neo-medieval style.

Halászbástya★ (Fisherman's Bastion) – *Behind Matthias Church. fishermansbastion.com. Access 1st floor mid-Mar–end Apr, 9am–7pm; beg May–mid-Oct, 9am–8pm (evenings after 8pm no charge). Ft1,000. Mid-Oct–mid-Mar 24hrs (no charge).* A series of splendid neo-Romanesque parapets and balconies with seven towers that symbolize the seven Magyar tribes. A walk along the terraces here is one the city highlights, with beautiful **views**★★ of

the Danube and Pest. You can linger and enjoy the panorama with a cup of coffee in the café under the arcades.

Looking towards Pest

Széchenyi Lánchíd★★ (Chain Bridge) – *C5*. Guarded by two stone lions at either end, the city's oldest bridge is also the most famous. Built between 1839 and 1849, it has a span of 380m/1,247ft and a width of 15.7m/51ft 6in. The skilful use of stone and iron combines to create a fine classical structure, which is even more beautiful when lit up at night.

Danube Promenade★★ – *D5–6*. This broad path hugs the left (east) bank of the river from Széchenyi tér to Petőfi tér, where a statue of the poet Sándor Petőfi stands in front of the Marriott Hotel. The backdrop to the promenade is the most beautiful panorama in Budapest, with the view over the Danube, the Chain Bridge, Elizabeth Bridge, Buda Castle and Gellért Hill. The spectacle is even more dazzling at night.

GELLÉRTHEGY★★

(Gellért Hill)
CD7 Access: Ⓜ *1 Opera* 🚊 *19, 41, 47, 48, 56, 56A Szent Gellért tér. To get here on foot from Pest, cross Liberty Bridge.*

Szabadság híd★★ (Liberty Bridge, 1896). Look out for the turul birds on top of the portals at either end. There are a number of thermal springs in the wooded Gellért Hill area, which explains why the well-known Gellért Gyógyfürdő (thermal baths) are located here (*☞see p. 86*).

LIPÓTVÁROS★★★

(Leopold Town)
CD3–4 Acces: Ⓜ *2 Kossuth Lajos tér;* 🚋 *2 Kossuth Lajos tér.*
This area is named after Leopold II, king of Hungary for a brief time only, 1790–92. Together with Belváros, it forms part of the historic centre of Pest and is where you will find the Parliament Building and St. Stephen's Basilica, among other iconic sights. Close by is tree-lined Falk Miksa Street with its grand buildings and antique shops perfect for browsing.

Országház★★★
(Parliament Building)
C3 Kossuth Lajos tér 1–3. Ⓜ *2 Kossuth Lajos tér.* 📞 *(1) 441 4904.*

latogatokozpont.parlament.hu. Buy tickets from the Visitor Centre, to the right of the building (access via the lower ground floor). Open Apr–Oct, 8am–6pm; Nov–Mar, 8am–4pm. Closed during plenary sessions and public holidays. Ft3,500 for citizens of the EU on presentation of ID, Ft6,700 for non-EU citizens. Tours in English at 10am, noon, 12.30pm, 1.30pm, 2.30pm, 3.30pm.
👤 Visitor numbers are limited. It's best to buy your ticket online at: jegymester.hu/parlament (an extra charge of Ft290 if you buy them on the spot on the day).
Designed by Imre Steindl, this vast neo-Gothic building is reminiscent of the UKs' Houses of Parliament or Milan's Cathedral, with its series of arcades, galleries and pinnacles, and dome and bell towers. Part is open to the public. Mounting the sumptuous

Great Staircase, you reach the huge Domed Hall, where you can see the **Crown Jewels ★★**, the **Old Upper House Hall** and its **lobby** containing statues of allegories of the trades, gilded decoration and chandeliers.

Magyar Szecesszió Háza★
(House of Hungarian Art Nouveau)
D3–4 Honvéd utca 3. Ⓜ *2 Kossuth Lajos tér, or 3 Arany János utca;* 🚋 *2 Kossuth Lajos tér.* 📞 *(1) 269 46 22. magyarszecessziohaza.hu. Open Mon–Sat, 10am–5pm. Ft2,000.*
Unique in Hungary, this museum pays hommage to the Art Nouveau style. It is located in a house that belonged to the art-collecting Bedő family, an Art Nouveau jewel in itself. Paintings, furniture and decorative objects compete for space ove three floors; the effect is a little more antique shop than museum, but well worth visiting.

Szabadság tér★
(Liberty Square)
D4 Ⓜ *3 Arany János utca.*
A spacious square bordered by buildings with majestic exteriors. The controversial Memorial to the Victims of the German Invasion (2014) is in the southern section; its detractors denounce it as a 'falsification of history', believing it minimizes the country's responsibility in the deportation of Jews and the Romani people.

Postatakarékpénztár ★★
(Former Postal Savings Bank)
D4 Hold utca 4. Ⓜ *3 Arany János utca; bus 15, 115 Hold utca.*
Designed by Ödön Lechner (1845–1914), a pioneer and key exponent of

Hungarian Art Nouveau (also known as Secessionism). The result is quite dazzling.

Szent István Bazilika★★
(St. Stephen's Basilica)
D4 Szent István tér. Ⓜ 1 Bajcsy-Zs. út, or Ⓜ 1 and 2 Deák Ferenc tér. bazilika. biz. Open Mon–Fri, 9am–5pm; Sat 9am–1pm, Sun 1pm–5pm (no charge). Construction of the basilica took 55 years and was completed in 1906, with Miklós Ybl taking over from József Hild on the latter's death in 1867. The result is a massive church in the neo-Renaissance style. The door of the main portal is decorated with the carved heads of the 12 apostles. Several statues by Leó Fessler can be seen parading around the exterior, while the interior is very grand and ornate. The Chapel of the Holy Dexter displays one of the most important of the basilica's possessions, a relic said to be the mummified right hand of King St. Stephen (👆*see p. 58*), which is carried in procession on 20 August, St. Stephen's Day.

Körpanoráma (North tower) – O*pen 10am–4.30pm (6.30pm in summer). Ft1,000.* Climb up for a fine **panoramic view**★★.

BELVÁROS★★

(The Inner City)
D5–7 Access: Ⓜ 3, 4 Kálvin tér, or Ⓜ 3 Ferenciek tere.
Belváros is part of Pest's historic centre. Its pedestrian streets are ideal for shopping, especially **Váci utca**★, lined with all kinds of stores and handy bureaus de change.

Magyar Nemzeti Múzeum★★
(Hungarian National Museum)
E6 Múzeum krt. 14-16. Ⓜ *3, 4 Kálvin tér.* 📞 *(1) 338 2122. mnm.hu/en. Open Tue–Sun, 10am–6pm. Closed public holidays. Ft2,600 (free with the Budapest card). Themed audioguides in English Ft750 from the museum shop.* Founded in 1802 by Count Ferenc Széchenyi, the museum occupies a neo-classical palace. Although the crown jewels are on display in the Parliament Building (👆*see p. 20*), part of the coronation regalia – the magnificent Byzantine coronation mantle, embroidered with gold and silk – is kept here. It was a gift from King Stephen I and Queen Gisela to the Church of the Virgin (now the basilica) in Székesfehérvár (👆*see p. 58*). The museum's collection covers the entire history of the country from the arrival of the Magyar tribes to the post-Communist era. It is well illustrated with maps and plans, paintings, art and everyday objects, weapons, furniture, clothing and film.

ERZSÉBETVÁROS★

(Old Jewish Quarter)
E5 Access: Ⓜ 2 Astoria.
Bordered by Károly körút, Erzsébet körút, Dohány utca and Király utca, this area is now the haunt of Budapest's young people, who crowd into the 'ruin bars' *(romkocsma)* here in the evenings, the dilapidated buildings in which fashionable clubs and bars have blossomed to produce a lively nightlife.

21

Dohány utcai Zsinagóga★★
(Dohány Street Synagogue)

Dohány utca 2. Ⓜ *2 Astoria, trolleybus 74 Nagy Diófa utca.* ℰ *(1) 413 5584. jewishtourhungary. com. Open May–Sept, 10am–8pm (Fri, 4pm); Mar, Apr & Oct, 10am–6pm (Fri 4pm); Nov–Feb, 10am–4pm (Fri, 2pm). Closed Sat & Jewish holidays. Ft5,000.*
The largest synagogue in Europe was completed in 1859. Byzantine and Moorish in influence, it is a beautiful building made of coloured bricks, with two towers topped by onion domes.

ANDRÁSSY ÚT★★

(Andrássy Avenue)

D5–F2 Access: Ⓜ *line 1, the first metro line in Continental Europe (1896). In spite of its venerable age, line 1 takes just 10min to get from the city centre to Városliget (City Park, ☙see p. 24). Bus 105 also serves the whole avenue.*

The most elegant thoroughfare in the capital, Andrássy út is sometimes known as the Budapest Champs-Élysées. Listed as a Unesco World Heritage Site in 2002, it is bordered by beautiful buildings littered with decorative mosaics, statues and carved friezes.
After a succession of notable buildings (high-end luxury stores, the State Opera House, the Liszt and Kodály museums...), this long, broad avenue turns into a chic residential street where beautiful villas and luxurious mansions stand side by side. Look out for statues of four of Hungary's great heroes in the central segments of Kodály körönd.

Magyar Állami Operaház★★
(Hungarian State Opera House)

E4 Andrássy út 22. Ⓜ *1 Opera.* ℰ *(30) 781 2630. opera.hu. Guided tours in English daily at 2pm, 3pm & 4pm. Ft2,500 (short concert included).*
One of the most prestigious opera houses in Europe. It was completed in 1884 and designed by Miklós Ybl in a neo-Renaissance style. On either side of the entrance, two niches house statues of the great Hungarian composers Franz Liszt and Ferenc Erkel. The interior is sumptuous: the grand staircase, the foyer, the smokers' corridor, the auditorium (ceiling frescoes by Károly Lotz), the reception room, the main staircase resplendent with gilding and marble.

Terror Háza★★
(House of Terror Museum)

E3 Andrássy út 60. Ⓜ *1 Vörösmarty utca.* 🚊 *4, 6 Oktogon.* ℰ *(1) 374 2600. terrorhaza.hu. Open Tue–Sun, 10am–6pm. Closed public holidays. Ft3,000. Not suitable for children.*
This building is not just a museum, it bears witness to two tragic periods in the history of Hungary. In 1944 it was the headquarters of the Hungarian Nazis and from 1945 to 1956 it was the headquarters of the AVO and ÀVH, the Communist secret police. Today, its role is to recall the terrible acts carried out by the dictatorships and to act as a memorial that pays tribute to the victims of terror.

Liszt Ferenc Emlékmúzeum★
(Franz Liszt Memorial Museum)

F3 Vörösmarty utca. ℰ *(1) 322 9804. lisztmuseum.hu. Open Mon–Fri,*

22

Széchenyi Baths

10am–6pm, Sat 9am–5pm. Closed Sun & public holidays. Ft2,000. Audioguide in English Ft700.

A reconstruction of the small service apartment in the old Academy of Music building, in which Franz Liszt lived during the last five years of his life, when staying in Budapest. In the bedroom, office and living room, you can see furniture, books and objects belonging to the great composer, including the Bösendorfer piano that was his favourite.

☺ A concert takes place every Saturday at 11am (included in the ticket price).

VÁROSLIGET★★

(City Park)
G1–2 Access: Ⓜ *1 Hősök tere.*
Popular throughout the year, families come here to wander its paths in search of shade in summer and to enjoy skating in winter, or Szechenyi Baths at any time of year, which are among the most beautiful in Budapest.

Hősök tere
(Heroes' Square)
G2 This huge square, designed by the architect Albert Schickedanz, has the Museum of Fine Arts on one side and the Hall of Art on the other. In the centre is the tall column of the **Millennium Monument★**, which commemorates the one thousandth anniversary (1896) of the Magyar conquest. Behind it two colonnades are peopled with statues. Heroes' Square has a long history as a great assembly point for public events, celebrations and festivities.

Szépművészeti Múzeum★★★
(Museum of Fine Arts)
FG1–2 Dózsa György út 41 (Hősök tere). Ⓜ *1 Hősök tere.* ℘ *(1) 469 7100. szepmuveszeti.hu. Open Tue–Sun, 10am–6pm, ticket office closes at 5pm. Closed Mon. Ft3,200.*

The museum occupies a vast neo-classical building behind a portico consisting of eight Greek-inspired Corinthian columns. Head to the basement to see art from the various eras of Ancient Egypt. The ground floor houses Greek and Roman antiquities, while the first and second floors display masterpieces of European painting (1260–1600), from Titian to Rubens, and Hungarian art (1600–1800).

Széchenyi Gyógyfürdő★★★
(Széchenyi Baths)
G1 Állatkerti krt. 11. Ⓜ *1 Széchenyi fürdő.* ♿See p. 87 opening times.
Said to be one of the largest thermal complexes in Europe, the baths are a neo-Baroque profusion of cherubs and statues languishing in the sun. People come here to spend the day as a family, relax with friends, play chess while half immersed in the water and splash around in the dozen or so indoor pools, including an underwater traction pool. There's something for everyone. Outside are more pools, including a large pool with whirlpools, a swimming pool for 'normal' swimming, a hot bath (38°C/100°F) and naturist areas on the terraces, not forgetting a restaurant. It is even more extraordinary in winter, when snow covers the ground and clouds of steam drift across the pools like a

scene from a fairy tale. The Széchenyi springs, discovered in 1868–78, are the deepest and warmest in the city at a temperature of 75°C/167°F.

ALSO SEE

Iparművészeti Múzeum★★
(Museum of Applied Arts)
F7 Üllői út 33–37. Ⓜ *3 Corvin-negyed. imm.hu. Closed for renovation work until end 2020.*
Inaugurated in 1896 (for the country's millennium celebrations), this building by Ödön Lechner typifies the Secessionist style and its Eastern influence.This is most evident on the roofs and facades in the colourful ceramic decoration with floral and animal motifs. The interior is less colourful but still striking. A large hall beneath a glass atrium has a mezzanine floor around the perimeter, bordered by columns, arches and balustrades. The collection includes a wealth of European Arts and Crafts objects in five categories: porcelain, ceramics, glassware; paper making, leather, bookbinding, decorated paper; textiles; wood, carpentry, cabinet making; metal and ironwork.

Nagy Vásárcsarnok★★
(Great Market Hall)
E7 Vámház krt. 1–3. Ⓜ *4 Fővám tér. piaconline.hu. Open Mon, 6am–5pm; Tue–Fri, 6am–6pm; Sat 6am–3pm.*
This large building with its brick exterior, neo-Gothic towers, majolica-covered roof and clock looks more like a railway station than a market hall. But inside there's no mistaking

its purpose. The ground floor is full of stalls selling fruit and vegetables, strings of paprika and huge salamis. Upstairs, on the gallery running around the perimeter, you'll find bars and stalls selling food, handicrafts and Hungarian wines and spirits.

Margitsziget★★
(Margaret Island)
CD1 Access: southern end of the island 🚋 *4, 6 Margitsziget/Margit híd; HÉV 5 Margit híd;* Ⓜ *3 Nyugati pályaudvar. Northern end:* 🚋 *1 Népfürdő utca/ Árpád híd. On the island itself:* 🚍 *26.*
A peaceful, green space that is closed to traffic, the island is the place to come for relaxing or playing sport. Look out for the Centennial Memorial, the Palatinus Baths, the ruins of the convent where Princess Margaret lived (daughter of King Béla IV, to whom the island owes its name), Artists' Promenade, the old water tower, the open-air theatre and the musical fountain.

Ludwig Múzeum Budapest★★
(Ludwig Museum of Contemporary Art)
Off map Komor Marcell utca 1. HÉV 7 Közvágóhíd. 🚋 *1, 2 Közvágóhíd.* ℘ *(1) 555 3444. www.ludwigmuseum. hu. Open Tue–Sun, 10am–6pm. Ft1,600 permanent collection.*
Definitely not to be missed if you are interested in modern art (especially Pop art). Great international artists represented here include Roy Lichtenstein, Jean Tinguely, Frank Stella and Joseph Beuys. It also holds excellent temporary exhibitions.

Lake Balaton and around★★★

Should you head for the north or the south shore? They are quite different in character. On the north-east shore, in the town of Balatonfüred, for example, there is a timeless quality. Baroque churches, Art Nouveau pavilions, elegant residential villas, colourful wooden cabins mounted on stilts and fragrant gardens extend down to the shore and then west to the nearby Tihany Peninsula. However, at Badacsony, just a few miles further on, the atmosphere changes. This is still the north shore, but now the backdrop consists of strangely beautiful hills, this is the land of wine-growers and open-air restaurants. Walkers come here to explore the area's unusual geology and its thermal springs. The south shore, on the other hand, is all about family holidays, sunshine, all-inclusive hotels and small lakeside resorts. During high season both shores are very busy and finding accommodation in the larger towns becomes a little more difficult. If you want peace and quiet, the villages can be a better choice, as in summer Hungarians come from all over the country to relax and swim in the lake. The shallow waters of the south shore are perfect for families, too, while confident swimmers are more likely to head to the north shore, where the lake bed shelves more steeply only a little way out.

▶**Location:** The resort town of Balatonfüred, the gateway to the north Balaton area (Siófok performs the same honours for the southern shore), is 130km/81mi south-west of Budapest by the M7 highway. The lake extends 77km/48mi from east to west, while its width varies from 14km/8.6mi to 1.5km/1 mile between the Tihany Peninsula on the north shore and Szántód on the south (the two are linked by ferry). The M7 runs along the south shore and Rte 71 along the north. Both roads are in excellent condition.

▶**Info:** Every town, or almost every town, has a tourist office *(Tourinform)*. The principal offices are at: **Balatonalmádi** (*Városház tér 4;* ℘ *(88) 594 081; open 8am–4pm, Sat 10am–5pm, Sun 10am–2pm;* **Balatonfüred** *(p. 34)*; **Tihany** *(p. 38)*; **Badacsony region** *(p. 44)*; **Siófok** (*Fő tér 11, in the base of the water tower;* ℘ *(84) 696 236; open Mon–Fri 8am–6pm, Sat 9am–1pm.*

▶**Tip:** In low season, it is worth checking out accommodation and restaurants before you travel. A number close at the end of September when the water in the lake starts to cool, although there is still plenty going on in the area in early autumn. As a general rule, everything starts to open again in May when it becomes possible to swim in the lake once more.

Detachable map AB6–7 to EF3.
♿ *See Addresses pp. 69, 76, 81, 85, 87 and 88.*

THE NORTH SHORE★★

A stretch of 111km/69mi heading west from Balatonalmádi. From Budapest, leave the M7 highway at junction 90 (direction Balatonfüred), and follow Rte 71, which passes the eastern end of the lake.

The shore is peppered with lakeside resorts, while vineyards cling to the volcanic slopes that produce some very pleasant white wines.

BALATONALMÁDI

E3–4 Dominated by Balatonakarattya cliff, this is the first major resort you come to on the lake's north shore, approaching from Budapest and the east. In summer its beaches and sailing clubs are buzzing with activity. From the town centre, brown signs marked *Óvári-kilátó* direct you to its highest point *(about 2.5km/1.5mi by car)*, where an **observation tower** *(kilátó)* provides a stunning view of the lake. It is the first of a series of resorts offering panoramic views, since one of the attractions of the north shore is its rolling countryside. Hills sit to the rear, like a series of balconies overlooking the lake and its water that changes colour with the weather.

If you have time, stop off to see the very pretty **Erődített Református templom** *(Reformed Church – Veszprémi u. 107; take the right turn Magtár u. off Rte 71, turn left at the top, then first right at St. Ignác templom).* Encircled by a wall, it dates from the 11C and 12C and is one of Hungary's oldest village churches.

👥 If you feel like a swim, head to the private **Wesselényi Strand**, (half-grass, half-sand beach). It also benefits from some shade and is well equipped with play areas and sun loungers *(Szent István sétány 6; open 15 May–15 Sept, 8.30am–11.30pm; Ft900, children Ft600).*

FELSŐÖRS

E4 Set back a little from the lake, this village, with its small **Római katolikus plébániatemplom** (Roman Catholic Parish Church, 13C), is reason enough to explore here. It's a pleasant drive through the vineyards and stone quarries that give the houses their distinctive colours: black from basalt and volcanic rock, white from limestone and red from sandstone. 🍷 The local wine-making tradition dates back to when the Romans planted vines in the region (1C–4C). *Return to Rte 71, which follows the shoreline around the lake.*

BALATONFÜRED★

E4 🕐*See p. 34.*
Continue on Rte 71. When you arrive at the foot of Tihany Peninsula, the road makes a slight detour.

TIHANY★★★

E5 🕐*See p. 38.*
🍷 To get to the south shore, catch the ferry at the end of the peninsula *(15min crossing, p. 104).* The queue builds up quickly in summer but crossings are frequent. Nearby eateries help to pass the time waiting.

ÖRVÉNYES

D5 Apart from its water mill, which is still working *(Szent Imre utca 3)*, this neat little village with its white houses is worth a stop for its small grass beach equipped with facilities *(Platán Szabadstrand, Fürdő utca)*. Shaded by trees, lifeguards patrol in summer *(July–20 Aug, 10am–8pm, no charge)*. Pedalos, windsurf boards, kayaks and dinghies can be hired and there is a nice view of Tihany Peninsula.

BALATONUDVARI

D5 Just to the right of the main road as you enter the village, stop off to look at the cemetery *(temető)*, which has some unsusual heart-shaped tombstones (late 18C–early 19C). **Fövenyes strand** (beach) here has lovely shallow water, making it ideal for families. And if you're still here as night falls, you can while away a warm summer's evening watching a film – they have an outdoor cinema here 1 June–30 August *(every evening at 9pm, Ft1,000/person)*.

BADACSONY★★★

C6 See p. 44.

KÁLI BASIN★

C5 See p. 45.

SZIGLIGETI VÁR★

(Szigliget Castle)
B6 Signposted from the entrance to the village. Parking at the foot of the castle. www.szigligeti-var.hu. Open

Jul–Aug, 8am–8pm; May & June, 9am–7pm; Apr & Sept, 9am–6pm; Mar & Oct, 9am–5pm; rest of the year, 10am–4pm. Ft800 (6–18 yrs Ft400). There's a climb up to the castle – a paved path through woodland, then a flight of steps leads to the top of **Várhegy** (Castle Hill, 239m/784ft), on top of which the 13C castle is perched. It escaped the attentions of the Turkish invaders, but was eventually destroyed by the Habsburgs. However, it retains enough of its original features to give an idea of how splendid it once was. The view from the top is across ancient volcanic hills, now covered with vineyards, to the lake and the village below. Although it is hard to imagine today, this was once an island ('szigliget' means 'small island'). There are some swings and other amusements for children. In summer displays by people in costume (combat, traditional dancing, falconry...) take the castle back to its medieval heyday. Concerts are also held here on some evenings.

A shop selling home-made ice cream, regularly ranked among the best in Hungary, lies at the foot of the path leading up to the castle. The pistachio flavour is one of the most popular.

HÉVÍZ THERMAL LAKE★★★

A6 See p. 48.

KESZTHELY★★

A6 See p. 50.

THE SOUTH SHORE

*123km/76.5mi from Keszthely.
Follow Rte 71.*
'What is the south shore's biggest
attraction? Its view of the north
shore!' So goes a local joke that
is turned on its head by the many
visitors who come here to enjoy the
south shore's lively atmosphere.
Its string of resorts teems with
people during the summer, when the
shoreline becomes one huge lakeside
playground. There is a good choice
of accommodation, from basic to
high-end, with eateries ranging from
traditional inns serving Hungarian
dishes to bistros offering food with a
modern twist, run by young chefs.
You can also step back from the lake
a little and wander the surrounding
leafy country lanes to discover
charming old farmhouses with roofs
thatched with reeds, typical of this
lake region and still resisting the
pressures of tourism.
*At Fonyód, take Rte 6701 towards
Kaposvàr.*

SZENT EGYED BENCÉS APÁTSÁG ROMJAI, AT SOMOGYVÁR★

(Ruins of the Benedictine Abbey)
*Besliahegy 64. ℘ (70) 197 9902.
Visitor Centre: open June–Aug,
10am–6pm; check times for rest of the
year. Ft1,200.*
C8 As a break from the lakeside
resorts, make a detour inland to see
the ruins of a Benedictine abbey
tucked away in the Hungarian
countryside. In 1091 King Ladislas I
asked the Benedictine monks at the

Abbey of St. Gilles (Szent Egyed, in
Hungarian) in France to establish
this monastery. From the ruins that
remain, it is possible to get an idea
of the size of the church, which was
60m/197ft long and 24m/79ft wide.
*Make a U-turn to rejoin Rte 71 towards
Siófok.*

BALATONBOGLÁR★

D6 This village of 6,200 inhabitants,
typical of the south shore's lakeside
resorts, has a line of grass and sand
beaches bordered by numerous
places offering various types of
accommodation. Long, tree-lined
avenues run beside the lake, while
beautiful houses are set back a little
under the trees.
Gömbkilátó★ (Sphere Lookout) –
*Kilátó utca. ℘ (30) 351 4476.
Parking (charges apply). Open
summer, 9am–9pm; check times
for rest of the year. Ft300 (3–18 yrs
Ft250).* 👥 Looking very similar to
the Atomium in Brussels (a 1950s
futuristic building), this unusual
lookout sits high up inside a sphere
constructed from 240 steel triangles.
It affords a fine view of the lake
and the hills on the north shore.
Illuminated at night, it is one of Lake
Balaton's iconic sights.
👥 The wooded hill on which the
lookout stands is now an adventure
park with a treetop rope course,
go-karts, a café-restaurant, bouncy
castles and other attractions during
the summer season.
*Continue on Rte 71 for 28km/17.5mi,
passing through Balatonlelle and
Balatonszemes.*

SZÁNTÓD

E5 This lakeside resort has the distinction of being at the narrowest point of the lake, just 1.5km/1 mile from the north shore. The ferry to cross over to Tihany Peninsula opposite is based here (♿see p. 38).

Szántódpuszta Majormúzeum★ (Szántódpuszta Tourist and Cultural Centre) – *Signposted from the town centre.* ℘ *(30) 447 82 16. szantodpuszta.hu. Open Jun–Aug, 8.30am–6pm; mid-Apr–end May, check times (closed Sept–mid Apr). Ft900.*

👥 With its well-restored rural 18C and 19C buildings, this large wooded park is also an open-air museum. Linked by shaded pathways, some of the buildings house small exhibitions depicting life on a farm. There are animal enclosures with calves, cows and pigs, and an aquarium where you can get acquainted with the different fish living in Lake Balaton. Horseriding and trips in horse-drawn carriages are also available.

Return to Rte 71 and continue for 15km/9.5mi.

Between Szántód and Siófok, it is almost impossible to tell where one resort ends and the next begins. Out of season they are deserted, but in the summer they are packed.

SIÓFOK★

EF5 Nestling in a hollow between two rocky peaks, this lakeside resort has a main beach that attracts as many as 13,500 visitors a day. Popular with families, it is also a meeting place for young Hungarians who come for its music concerts and late-night bars and clubs, which together have erased almost all trace of its original old-world, middle-class elegance.

Víztorony (Water Tower) – *Fő tér 11. viztorony.com. Open June–Sept, Tue–Sun, 9am–midnight; check times for rest of year. Ft850 (children Ft350).*

👥 Built entirely of concrete in 1912, this 45m/147.5ft high monument has become the town's landmark. The base houses the tourist office and a lift that will take you to the top, where you will find a lookout point and revolving café with panoramic views.

Kálmán Imre Emlékház (Emmerich Kálmán Memorial Home) – *Kálmán Imre sétány 5 . ℘ (84) 311287. emlekhaz.konyvtar-siofok.hu. Open Tue–Fri, 10am–5pm; Sat, 9am–1.30pm, (closed Sun & Mon). Ft500.* The house itself where Imre (Emmerich) Kálmán (1882–1953), composer of operettas such as *The Gay Hussars/Autumn Manoeuvres*, was born no longer exists, but the town has opened a museum in his memory here at no. 5. You can see his music scores and other personal items. As a Jew, he was forced to flee from the Nazis to the United States in 1940.

Two very different buildings in Siófok will appeal to those interested in architecture: **Ezüstpart Hotel** *(Liszt Ferenc sétány 4; 4km/2.5mi west of the centre),* a distinctive building from the 1970s, and the **Evangélikus templom** (Evangelical Church), built in the Organic style, with an entrance designed to look like a giant owl *(Fő utca 220, Oulupark; 10min walk from the centre).*

AROUND LITTLE BALATON★

A7–8 **Kis-Balaton** (Little Balaton) became separated from the main lake following the build-up of alluvium from the Zala river, which formed a kind of natural dam in the late 18C. With its 3,500ha/8,649 acres of reedbeds dotted with shallow pools, this is a peaceful haven. Renowned for the richness of its bird life, it is now a protected nature reserve.

ZALAKAROS★

A8 36km/22mi south-west of Keszthely by Rtes 75 and then 7522.
👥 Regarded as a jewel among the many Hungarian thermal spa towns, this quiet little place has been subjected to massive development since the discovery of a hot spring here in 1962. The original **thermal baths** are in the middle of a gigantic water park where there are treatment pools but also, as is common in this type of complex, around sixty attractions for all the family, including water slides, pools with wave machines and jaccuzis (⚅*see p. 87*). It is especially popular with Czech, Austrian and German visitors.

KÁPOLNAPUSZTA BUFFALO RESERVE AND LAKE

A8 10km/6mi north-east of Zalakaros. ℘ (70) 228 2864. bfnp.hu/en/buffalo-reserve-kapolnapuszta. Open daily, Apr & May, Sept & Oct 9am–5pm; Jun–Aug, 9am–6pm; Nov–Mar, 9am–4pm. Ft800 (3–14 yrs Ft500).

👥 Hungary's buffaloes are bred from the same domestic species as Italy's Campania buffaloes (whose milk is used to produce mozzarella). Once through the reception building you can see these impressive beasts, which have a liking for wallowing in mud baths, from a walkway that runs for about 1km/1.2mi. Rides in horse-drawn carriages are available *(Ft1,000, child Ft500)*.

KÁNYAVÁRI-SZIGET★

(Kányavári Island)
A8 7km/4.5mi north-west of Kápolnapuszta.
👥 This small island is the only part of the protected area of Kis-Balaton that can be visited by the public. After parking your car *(charges apply)* take the wooden footbridge (beneath semi-circular arches) over the reedbeds. The shaded paths lead to a lookout tower, play areas for children, small beaches and designated picnic areas under the trees. A peaceful place amid delightful countryside.

KIS-BALATON HÁZ

(Little Balaton House)
10km/6mi north-west of Kányavári Island. Vársziget, 8392 Zalavár. ℘ (83) 710 002. kisbalaton.hu. Open Tue–Sun, 15 Mar–15 Nov, 10am–6pm (1–15 Nov, 5pm). Closed Mon except during school holidays (no charge).*
👥 An interesting and informative visitor centre with a reconstruction of a marshy landscape, regional history, live webcam footage of Balaton's animal life and interactive exhibits.

Balatonfüred★

*This charming and elegant spa town has been patronized by
the great and the good of Hungarian high society for more than two hundred
years. Although water cures are available at the local cardiology hospital, the
spa water is an alkaline mineral water and not classed as medicinal. By the early
19C, the town already had several hotels and was a noted cultural centre with its
own theatre. It also had a port at which the first steamships on the lake would
call in. People would come here for spa treatments, interspersed with bathing
in the lake and a therapy based on its mud. Since then, this pretty little town
has learned how to move with the times and is now a centre for water sports
and sailing in particular. In the restaurants young chefs have discovered that
it is the ideal setting in which to showcase their talents, sweeping it along in a
gastronomic revival.*

▶**Location:** Arriving by car, allow 1hr 15min from Budapest Airport, taking first
the M7 highway and then, at Balatonvilágos, the north-east fork in the road
towards Balatonfüred on Rte 71. **By train:** 1 direct train per hour from Budapest
Déli station, which is also the M2 metro terminus *(journey time 2hrs, Ft2,800,
mavcsoport.hu/en).* **By bus:** direct from outside Budapest's Népliget metro
station *(journey time 2hrs 45min, Ft2,800, see volanbusz.hu/en).* ⏍*See p 3.*
▶**Info: Tourist Office** – *Blaha Lujza utca 5. ℘ 461 210. Open in summer, Mon-
Sat, 9am–7pm (Sun, 10am–4pm); check times for the rest of the year.*
▶**Tip:** Balatonfüred is an ideal base for water sports. The resort is home to the
country's oldest yacht club and is well equipped for all things nautical.
Detachable map E4.
⏍ See *Addresses pp. 70, 77, 81, 85 and 89.*

Balatonfüred's reputation owes a
great deal to the actress and singer
dubbed 'the nation's nightingale',
Lujza Blaha (1850–1926). She often
stayed here, attracted by its gentle
climate, sheltered by trees offering
protection from any cold winds
later in the season. The lovely early
19C architecture contributed to its
appeal, as did its association with
other notable figures of the time,
such as the poet Sándor Kisfaludy
and physician Dr. István Huray, who

worked at the hospital and helped to
modernize the town. Other celebrities
of the time had houses here, such as
writer Mór Jókai *(⏍see p. 36).*
The town has developed further since
then, but it has preserved its wide
avenues, shaded by mature trees
and fringed with beautiful villas and
elegant hotels.
Lake Balaton proved to be ideal
for sailing, an activity reportedly
introduced by a Briton at the end
of the 19C. It soon became popular,

Tagore Promenade, Balatonfüred

attracting both amateurs and experienced yachtsmen and women between May and November. Now not a day seems to pass in summer without some kind of race or regatta being held. The most prestigious, the Kékszalag (Blue Ribbon) in July, has been held since 1934 and attracts up to 500 different craft. It starts and finishes at Balatonfüred and completes a circumnavigation of the lake (♿ see p. 108).

TAGORE SÉTÁNY★

(Tagore Promenade)
All Balatonfüred comes out at dusk to stroll along this shaded promenade beside the lake, named in honour of the Indian writer and Nobel Laureate **Rabindranath Tagore** (1861–1941). Treated at the heart hospital here, in 1926 he planted the first tree (a linden) on the promenade in gratitude. His statue now stands proudly looking out over the lake.

Bodorka Balaton Aquarium

Tagore sétány 333. ☏ (20) 482 1283. bodorka.info.hu. Open Jul–Aug, daily, 9am–7pm; rest of the year, Wed–Sun, 10am–5pm. Ft1,000 (children Ft500).
👥 An ecocentre named after the Hungarian roach *(bodorka)*, a green fish with an orange tail that, along with the wels catfish (aka sheatfish), is abundant in the lake. The centre also explains the lake's history and monitors its natural resources with a view to conservation. Only a few years ago, 47 species of fish could be found in its waters. Today the number has dropped to just 24.

😊 At the western end of the promenade, the large yellow building (now home to the Vitorlás Restaurant, ♿ see p. 78) once housed Hungary's first yacht club. It has fine views from the terrace.

KEREKTEMPLOM

(Round Church)
Blaha Lujza utca.
Despite its appearance, perhaps inspired by the Pantheon in Rome, this church only dates back as far as the mid-19C. It has become a local landmark and appears on many of Balatonfüred's colourful souvenirs and postcards. In summer exhibitions are held in the basement.

JÓKAI EMLÉKHÁZ

(Jókai Memorial House)
Honvéd utca 1. ☏ 950 876. Open Wed–Sun, 10am–6pm. Ft650.
The lovely villa that once belonged to **Mór Jókai** (1825–1904) has been turned into his memorial house. A prolific novelist, he was very popular in Britain, where he was sometimes compared to Dickens and could count Queen Victoria among his fans. He wrote most of his work here.

VÁROSI MÚZEUM

(History Museum)
Blaha utca 3. ☏ 580 041. Open Wed–Sun, 10am–6pm. Ft650.
👥 At one time this attractive building belonged to the director of the thermal baths. It now houses a small, slightly dated but instructive

museum on the golden age of Balatonfüred, which became a spa town towards the end of the 18C. Among the exhibits are works of art and objects from everyday life (including a collection of glasses used by spa guests to take the water). Two of the rooms are dedicated to children, one of which contains antique toys.

GYÓGY TÉR★

Thanks to the **Kossuth Lajos Forrás** (Lajos Kossuth drinking water fountain), erected in 1800 in the centre of Gyógy tér (which translates as Cure Square), everyone – whether a spa guest or not – can sample Balatonfüred's sulphurous water between 1 May and 30 September. In the 18C, bitter water from carbonated springs was mixed with sheep's whey to treat stomach complaints. It was also used as a remedy for tuberculosis. The useful properties of the waters have been recognized since the end of the 19C, particularly in the treatment of heart disease.

SZANATÓRIUM

Gyógy tér 2.
The Szanatórium was erected in 1810 as a convalescent home and now houses the **State Hospital of Cardiology**. Beneath the arcades of this lovely old building, you will find commemorative plaques bearing the names of many famous intellectuals, artists and politicians (both Hungarian and from abroad), who were looked after here.

ANNA GRAND HOTEL

Gyógy tér 1.
The hotel is famous for having hosted the **Anna Ball**, the resort's glamorous star social event. It was first held in 1825 (*see p. 108*).

KISFALUDY STRAND

(Kisfaludy Beach)
Of the town's three beaches, we recommend **Kisfaludy Strand** *(entry fee charged in summer)*, which is clean and has good facilities *(balatonfuredistrandok.hu; open summer, 8.30am–7pm)*.

LÓCZY-BARLANG

(Lóczy Cave)
3km/2mi north of the town centre (5min by car or 30min walk). Öreghegyi út. (30) 491 0061. bfnp. hu/en/loczy-cave-balatonfured. Visit by guided tour only (about 30 min). Open mid-Mar–Sept, 10am–6pm. closed Oct–mid Mar. Ft600.
Named after Hungarian geologist Lajos Lóczy and carved out by limestone erosion, this cave is among the many unusual geological formations found in the region. It was discovered in 1882 and was first opened to the public in 1934.
A path starts outside the cave and leads to **Jókai-kilátó**, a lookout tower high above the trees *(open all year, free entry)*. It stands on top of Tamás Hill, adding to the hill's existing elevation of 317m/1,040ft. The views over the lake and to Balatonfüred and the Tihany Peninsula are superb.

Tihany★★★

This undulating wooded peninsula stretches five kilometres (three miles) out into the turquoise waters of Lake Balaton, towards the opposite shore. Peeping out above the trees are the twin towers topped with onion domes of Tihany Abbey, famous for its Rococo interior and its deed of foundation, the earliest surviving document written in old Hungarian. If you want to escape the summer crowds in the delightful small village of Tihany, you don't have to walk far before you find yourself in 400 hectares (988 acres) of Hungary's oldest nature reserve. It is famous for its hiking trails and unusual geological phenomena – geysers and strangely shaped basalt formations that are more typical of Iceland than Central Europe. In summer, the heady perfume of lavender adds an enchanted air to the whole setting.

▶**Location: By car** via Rte 71 (8km/5mi south-west of Balatonfüred and 39km/24mi north-east of Badacsony). **By train:** there is no service to Tihany itself, the nearest railway stations are at Örvényes and Balatonfüred. The latter has a good bus service to Tihany *(up to 20 buses per day in summer)* and – usefully – the buses stop at both the village and the ferry that operates all year round between Tihany and Szántód. Crossings are more frequent during high season, which helps avoid congestion on the roads *(balatonihajozas.hu; end June–beg Sept, 6.40am–11.20pm, every 40min; check times for rest of the year; Ft700/person, Ft400/bicycle, Ft1,900/car).*
▶**Info: Tourist Office:** *Kossuth Lajos utca 20. ℰ 538 104. bfnp.hu/en/tihany-peninsula-and-vicinity. Open Mon–Fri, 9am–5pm; Sat & Sun, 10am–4pm.*
▶**Tip:** The car parks around the centre soon get busy *(charges apply)*. Make sure you have change for the ticket machines.
Tihany Peninsula map p 41. Detachable map E5.
♿ See *Addresses pp. 71, 78, 81 and 89.*

THE VILLAGE

Situated approximately half way (2km/1.25 miles) inside the peninsula, on the far eastern side, the village is at the modest height of 80m/262ft. It dates back to the 11C when King András (Andrew) I founded the Benedictine Abbey. The village managed to resist successive attacks from the Turks and it was the Habsburgs who, in 1702, finally destroyed the castle, of which only ruins remain today.

You can climb up to the abbey by road from the main street, which is lined with souvenir shops.

Benedictine Abbey, Tihany

BENCÉS APÁTSÁG★★

(Benedictine Abbey)
℘ 538 200. tihanyiapatsag.hu.
Open summer, 9am–6pm, (Sun,
11.15am–6pm); check times rest of the
year. Ft1,200 (Ft800 out of season).
The two towers of this lovely old
abbey church are visible from quite a
distance. Founded in 1055 to serve as
a royal burial place, the tomb of **King
András I** lies in the crypt. However,
thanks to the vagaries of history, the
remains of András are the only royal
remains to be interred here, under
a simple white limestone slab. The
church itself dates from the 18C (the
original was destroyed in 1702). Its
rounded belltowers, tiled roofs and
amber colour lend it a distinctive
elegance, especially for a building
of such imposing dimensions. The
interior does not disappoint either,
displaying work by an Austrian
cabinetmaker and lay brother
Sebastian Stuhlhof, who created an
altar, sacristy and an exceptionally
fine organ in the Baroque and Rococo
styles of the time. From the cells of
the Benedictine monks, dug out of
the basalt hillside, it seems like a
sheer drop straight down into the
deep waters of the lake.
In the summer you might be able
to catch one of the **concerts** that
are organized at the abbey, often
featuring organ music.
Abbey Museum – *Combined ticket
with entrance to the abbey.* This small
museum is housed in an 18C building
next to the church. It includes an
exhibition on Charles IV, the last king
of Hungary (r. 1916–18), who was

detained in Tihany Abbey for a time
in 1921 after a failed attempt to be
restored to the throne.
🚶 If you have time before leaving,
walk around the building to the
viewpoint★★ on the left of the
church, as you face the lake.
Take the pretty footpath (Pisky
sétány), which heads off to the left
from the viewpoint. It leads to a
group of thatched houses that in
summer form a kind of small **open-air
museum** near some shops *(open May–
Sept, 10am–6pm; Ft800/600).*
Continue along Pisky sétány.

VISSZHANG-HEGY

(Echo Hill)
Signposted.
👥 The hill is famous for the echo
that at one time could be heard
reverberating around the hillside up
to 16 times. Shout in the direction of
Tihany Abbey and the words should
bounce off its northern wall. The
effect is less impressive these days
thanks to new building in the vicinity,
which has altered the acoustics, but
people still have fun trying it out.
*Before leaving the village to explore
the peninsula, retrace your steps down
the main street Kossuth Lajos utca.*

KOGART TIHANY

(Kogart Gallery)
*Kossuth Lajos utca 10. ℘ (30)
955 5958. kogarttihany.hu. Open
Jul–Aug, 10am–8pm; Apr–June &
Sept–Oct, 10am–6pm; rest of the year,
10am–4pm. Ft1,500 (children Ft750).*
Assembled by the collector Gábor

40

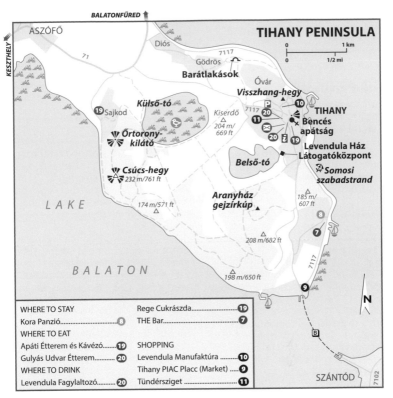

TIHANY PENINSULA

ASZÓFŐ

Diós

Gödrös

Barátlakások

Óvár

Visszhang-hegy

Külső-tó

Sajkod

Kiserdő
△ 204 m/
669 ft

TIHANY

Bencés
apátság

*Őrtorony-
kilátó*

**Levendula Ház
Látogatóközpont**

Csúcs-hegy
232 m/761 ft

Belső-tó

*Somosi
szabadstrand*

*Aranyház
gejzírkúp* ▲

174 m/571 ft

185 m/
607 ft

LAKE

△
208 m/682 ft

BALATON

△
198 m/650 ft

N

41

SZÁNTÓD

WHERE TO STAY	Rege Cukrászda......................**19**
Kora Panzió....................**8**	THE Bar...........................**7**
WHERE TO EAT	
Apáti Étterem és Kávézó........**19**	SHOPPING
Gulyás Udvar Étterem........**20**	Levendula Manufaktúra..........**10**
WHERE TO DRINK	Tihany PIAC Placc (Market).....**9**
Levendula Fagylaltozó........**20**	Tündérsziget......................**11**

Kovács, this private gallery's permanent collection highlights the work of Hungarian sculptor **Miklós Borsos** (1906–90), who spent every summer on the peninsula from 1943 onwards. Exhibitions of modern Hungarian art are also held here.
⊙ There are guided tours every Saturday in summer at 6pm (included in the entry ticket).

BARÁTLAKÁSOK

(Hermitage)
Óvár-hegy. North of Tihany village, ask for directions at the Tihany tourist office (♻p. 38).
Hidden away in thick woodland, these dwellings carved into the cliff face are not easy to find, but the path beneath the shade of the trees is very

pleasant, especially in summer. Greek Orthodox hermits are said to have lived here between the 12C and 14C and traces of their chapels can still be seen.

THE PENINSULA

The access road to Tihany village runs alongside a marshy area known as **Külső-tó** (outer lake). Further into the peninsula, fields of lavender grow around the larger **Belső-tó** (inner lake), which covers around 30ha/74 acres on a low plateau that stands 25m/82ft above Lake Balaton.

LEVENDULA HÁZ LÁTOGATÓKÖZPONT★

(Lavender House)
Major utca 67. ℘ 53 8033. bfnp.hu/en/lavender-house-visitor-centre-tihany. Open summer, 9am–6pm; check times for rest of the year. Ft1,200.
👥 This small visitor centre near Belső-tó presents a contemporary take on the history of the peninsula from its volcanic origins to the marshlands and lavender fields you see today. Activities such as a maze and a walkway beside the water add to the centre's interest for families.
🐣 You can pick your own bouquet of lavender in the adjoining field.

SOMOSI SZABADSTRAND

(Somosi Beach)
Somosi-öböl mellett. From Tihany village, head towards the port (the entrance to the beach is signposted on the left). ℘ (87) 538 030.
👥 Situated in the west of the

peninusla, this is actually a strip of concrete with steps down into the lake at intervals, but as it is a public beach entry is free. There are also toilet facilities, a café and parking *(charges apply)*.

ŐRTORONY-KILÁTÓ

(Őrtorony Lookout)
Mályva utca 19, Sajkod. Take the track to the lookout (signposted) at the end of Mályva utca, through the trees. ℘ (89) 513 100. No charge.
👥 Take Rte 71 which crosses Sajkod, a hamlet on the western side of the peninsula, where small houses are buried deep amid the greenery. At a height of 16.5m/54ft there are more great views, this time of Tihany Abbey and the Belső and Külső lakes.

WALKING TRAILS

👣 Explore the peninsula on foot via three well-marked paths; the tourist office can supply maps, but if you start to get lost, just look for the towers of Tihany Abbey peeping out above the trees to reorient yourself. One path runs beside a geyser field, a volcanic landscape where more than one hundred strange cone-shaped rock formations (such as the tallest, Aranyház, which means 'gold house') mark the locations of geysers that at one time shot out of the ground here; they were solidified following volcanic eruptions. Another path climbs to the top of **Csúcs-hegy** (Csúcs Hill, 232m/761ft) with its wonderful view★★ *(around a 2hr walk, leaving from the abbey).*

Benedictine Abbey and the Inner Lake, Lake Balaton in the background, Tihany Peninsula

Badacsony and around★★★

You can't miss the distinctive silhouette of Badacsony Hill, formed by an ancient volcano, with vineyards that tumble down its slopes towards Lake Balaton. Wine is very much a feature of the attractive landscape here, made from a number of different grape varieties that flourish on the terraces of basalt rock. Enjoy a stroll through the vineyards dotted with pretty houses belonging to the winemakers. The village of Badacsonytomaj is this small region's central point. It is served by rail and has a tourist office and plenty of accommodation, making it a good base during your visit. While you are here, be sure to climb to the top of Badacsony Hill (437m/1,434ft) to see the superb view. The partly paved road that leads up it is lined with wine cellars where, naturally, dropping in for a tasting is non-negotiable!

▶**Location: By car:** Rte 71 links the hamlets and villages along the lake. **By train:** the railway station is at Badacsonytomaj (on the internet, enter the name of the region, Badacsony): at least a dozen trains a day, *(journey time around 40min, for information and reservations see: mavcsoport.hu/en)*. **By bus:** a bus service operates between the principal sites May to August *(check at the tourist office for the exact route, which changes from year to year)*.
▶**Info: Tourist Offices** – **Badacsonytomaj** – *Park utca 14.* ✆ *(87) 531 013. Open Jul–Aug, Mon–Fri, 9am–7pm (Sat & Sun, 10am–7pm); check times for the rest of the year.* **Sümeg** – *Kossuth Lajos utca 15.* ✆ *550 276.*
Detachable map BD 4–6.
&♿ See *Addresses pp. 71, 78, 85 and 89.*

BADACSONY★★★

Badacsony is the name of both the region and the hill, whose volcanic rock gives the area its unique character. The many hamlets beside the lake follow the shore one after the other, almost forming one vast water sports resort.

Inland there are some good trails for walkers, with superb **views**★★ over the lake. One of the most popular (🥾 *3.2km/2mi*) is a relatively short but steep path to **Kisfaludy-kilátó** (Kisfaludy lookout), from where there is a stunning view of the lake and the surrounding countryside, including the strange volcanic rock formations. Along the way, wineries tempt you to pause for a tasting, most with terraces with panoramic views *(&♿ see p. 78)*. If the thought of the climb is a bit daunting, much of it can be covered by car.

SÜMEG★★

B4 *33km/20mi north-west of Badacsony on Rte 71, then Rte 84.*
The sight of this gorgeous little town, tucked away below a 13C castle sitting proudly on a promontory, certainly deserves to be on a postcard.

Sümegi vár (Sümeg Castle)★★
sumegvar.hu. Open summer, 9am–7pm; check times for rest of the year. Ft1,500 (6–14yrs Ft800).
👪 Hungarians come in their droves to see this castle, built as a symbol of national resistance to the Turks in the 16C and whose occupation it escaped. Visiting the castle more than compensates for the effort required to reach it, as much for the excellent historical reenactments that are staged as for the **views**★ it affords of Tapolca's extinct volcanoes. There is also a children's playground in the main courtyard.
Don't leave Sümeg without first taking a brief walk around the town. Its narrow streets are lined with attractive small houses. **Sümegi Római Katolikus templom** (Roman Catholic Parish Church, *Bíró Márton utca 3; open Mon–Sat, 8am–3.45pm*) is sometimes known as the 'Rococo

Sistine Chapel', with frescoes★★ by **Franz Anton Maulbertsch**, an Austrian painter whose work covers the walls of many 18C Hungarian churches. The Sistine Chapel comparison may be a little over the top, but the church is still a delight and very ornate.
🎭 In keeping with the medieval ambience, tournaments held in an arena at the foot of the castle are something of a local speciality, featuring participants in historical costume *(daily, mid-Jul–mid-Aug; Wed & Sat, rest of the year).*

KÁLI-MEDENCE★

(Káli Basin)
C5 *North-east of Badacsonytomaj.*
The 'Tuscany of Hungary', as this area is sometimes known, is a roughly diamond-shaped piece of land between **Salföld** *(9km/5.5mi east of Badacsonytomaj on Rte 71)* to the south and **Kapolcs** *(26km/16mi from Salföld on Rte 77)* to the north. It is filled with lavender fields, orchards and vineyards, and some unusual geological fomations, which have led to it being protected within the **Balaton-felvidéki Nemzeti Park** (Balaton Uplands National

A perfect 10 for Badacsony's wines
Hungary is renowned for its wines and those produced on the slopes of Badacsony since Roman times often feature among the best in the country. The combination of a Mediterranean-style microclimate and a subsoil of basalt creates a terroir on which highly regarded grape varieties thrive, such as Juhfark, Szürkebarát, Furmint and Kéknyelű. Badacsony produces a delicious local wine called Olaszrizling (which translates as 'Italian riesling'). You can also taste vintage wines in the many delightful whitewashed cellars that line the path that leads to the top of Badacsony Hill.

Park), a Unesco Global Geopark. An interpretive center at Salföld is under construction. It is an interesting area to explore, either along the dedicated nature trails *(guided tours: see bfnp. hu/en/guided-tours-in-kali-basin)*, or just wandering from village to village, especially as the quality of the restaurants has improved greatly over recent years, thanks to young chefs who have been buying up old farm buildings and are keen to revive the local cuisine (👍*see p. 71).*

Hegyestű Geológiai Bemutatóhely (Hegyestű Geological Visitor Site) – *at Hegyestű (between Monoszló and Zánka).* 📞 *555 294. bfnp.hu/ en/hegyestu-geological-visitor-site-monoszlo. Open summer, 9am–7pm; check times for the rest of the year. Ft800 (3–14yrs Ft500).* As well as providing a view of the old basalt quarry nearby, this small centre unravels the mysteries of the Upper Balaton area's geological heritage.

TAPOLCA

B5 13km/8mi north of Badacsony.
This small but picturesque spa town at the foot of **Szent György-hegy** (St. George's Hill) is in a lovely setting beside a lake fed by two underground springs that also have dug a cave system out of the rock. Part of the

caves lies beneath the local hospital and a nearby 4-star hotel. Some respiratory complaints can be treated here with speleotherapy, the breathing in of the dust-free, mineral-enriched air of the cave.

Tavas-barlang★ (Lake Cave) – *Kisfaludy utca 2.* 📞 *412 579. bfnp.hu/ en/tapolca-lake-cave-visitor-centre-tapolca. Open summer, 9am–8pm; check times for the rest of the year. Ft2,200 (3–14yrs Ft1,500).* 👥 Part of the impressive network of limestone tunnels under the town can be visited by boat, gliding along through the illuminated caves across the crystal clear subterranean water.

SOMLÓ-HEGY

(Somló Hill)
B2 38km/23.5mi north of Tapolca on Rte 8.
Welcome to the smallest wine region in Hungary, a few miles from the village of Somlójenő, on the slopes of Somló-hegy ('hat of God hill', 432m/1,417ft). Well known for its wine production, which was neglected during the Communist era, production (principally white) started here once more in the early 2000s.

🐾 **Climb Somló Hill** – If you do you'll find a great **view★** from Szent István-kilátó (lookout) on the top.

Ancient geological formations

The hills north of Lake Balaton tell a geological story dating back millions of years. Their conical shape derives from volcanic activity during the late Pannonic era – although the flattened tops of Badacsony, Szent György (St. George) and Csobánc hills make them look more like coffins. They are bordered by unusual basalt columns, the most striking being the Stone Gate of Badacsony and the basalt organ pipes of St. George's Hill.

Vineyards in the Badacsony region

Hévíz thermal lake★★★

(Hévízi-tó)

'Hé-víz' means 'hot water' and it is entirely thanks to its thermal lake that the village of Hévíz has become so famous. The lake is renowned throughout Europe and beyond for its therapeutic properties. Every year up to one million visitors make their way here for a treatment or just to bathe in its waters. The wooded setting and the pavilions mounted on stilts over the centre of the lake, covered in part by waterlilies, look very picturesque. In cold weather, hot gases and steam evaporate into the air, adding a mysterious, almost magical dimension, especially when the wild ducks that stop over here in winter take to the air with a beating of wings.

▶**Location:** Situated 10km/6mi north-west of the western end of Lake Balaton, Lake Hévíz is in the centre of a large wooded park, 500m/550yds south of the main pedestrianized street (Rákóczi utca).**By train:** Hévíz has no railway station, so rail travellers arrive at Keszthely Station (Mártírok utca), from where a frequent bus service takes them to Hévíz Bus Station *(15min)*.

▶**Info: Tourist Office:** *Rákóczi utca 2. ℘ 540 131. heviz.hu. Open Mon–Fri, 9am–5pm; Sat & Sun, 10am–3pm.* Information about the town, accommodation in Hévíz itself and nearby, and activities available in the area. Bicycle hire.
▶**Tip:** If you are interested in staying overnight as a spa guest, Hévíz has several 3 or 4 star hotels, some of which are accredited as thermal and/or therapeutic spas offering treatments. Otherwise, a useful alternative is to stay in Keszthely (ὥsee p. 50), which offers some attractive and less expensive accommodation, plus it has the added advantage of being accessible by train.
Detachable map A6.
ὥ See Addresses pp. 72 and 87.

Lake Hévíz, the largest thermal lake in the world, lies within a wooded park that is not open to the public. To visit the lake, you need to enter via the spa complex that manages it. Buy a 'visit only' ticket if you don't wish to bathe in the water, although it would be a shame to miss out on this experience. If you visit in September, you should see the waterlilies in flower.

HÉVÍZGYÓGYFÜRDŐ★★★

(Hévíz Thermal Spa)
Dr. Schulhof Vilmos utca 1. ℘ 342 830. spaheviz.hu. Open May–Aug, 8.30am–7pm; check times for rest of the year. Visit (no bathing) Ft1,000; with bathing Ft3,200 (3hrs), Ft3,900 (4hrs), Ft5,500 (day). Towel hire Ft400. There is a restaurant on site.

A little history

Popular since ancient times, the benefits of thermal bathing were recognized as long ago as the Stone Age! However, it was Count Festetics of Keszthely, owner of Keszthely and Hévíz, who really launched the town as a spa centre in 1795. Hévíz began to grow in popularity between the two world wars but really took off from 1970 onwards when a number of hotels were built, which mostly offered spa therapies but also dental and eye care. The main part of the Hévíz treatment involves bathing in the lake, together with various balneo and physical therapies, including the weight bath, developed by Hungarian rheumatologist Dr. Károly Moll and designed to help the spine.

With a surface area of 4.4ha/11 acres, the lake is fed by a spring producing 419 litres/108gals of water per second, enough to completely refresh the lake every 28 hours. Bathing is tempting whatever the season as the water temperature varies from 22°C/71°F in winter to 35–38°C/95–100°F in summer. The spring that feeds the lake emerges from a depth of 38m/124ft at a temperature of 38–42°C/95–107°F. During winter, a light cloud of steam rises above the water and can be seen from several miles away, prompting the locals to say that the lake is 'smoking its pipe'. Although the therapeutic properties of Lake Hévíz have been known for centuries, it first began to be developed on a large scale in the 18C, when the Festetics family who owned the land became involved. The complex you see today has a little of the fairytale palace about it, albeit a watery one. If you decide to bathe, you might like to follow the lead of many and use a flotation aid, so you can relax totally in and benefit from the warm water. They can be hired at the entrance (by the ticket office) or bought from one of the many shops that are nearby.

👁 Unless you have been given specific medical advice, bathing in the lake for more than 30 minutes is not recommended. Bathing is also not recommended for children under the age of 12. However, in the high season a special non-thermal swimming pool is reserved for them beside the lake.

Effects of the water

For visitors just passing through, bathing is fun, but for those seeking treatment the effects are as follows:
Physical – Since the water is warm, the body can be immersed without tensing up or experiencing a drop in temperature, so the muscles can relax. The hydrostatic pressure is excellent for the body's circulatory and lymphatic systems.
Chemical – Being balanced in negative and positive ions and other dissolved substances, the water is recommended for rheumatism, musculoskeletal conditions and similar disorders.
Peat from the lake bed – Slightly radioactive, the peaty mud of the lake floor contains various components, including organic compounds that have a mild antibacterial effect. Hence no pathogens can survive in the lake.

49

Keszthely★★

With its rows of traditional low houses and its charming small lanes lined with soft pastel-coloured facades, this small town has remained delightfully unspoilt, despite being one of the largest in the Lake Balaton region. Its reputation is mostly based on its Baroque palace, which was built for the Festetics, one of the grandest of the Hungarian aristocratic families, who were originally from Croatia. Construction began on this enormous building, the third largest in Hungary, in 1745 and continued for over a century. By 1945 it was one of the few such buildings to remain intact in the country, having escaped both destruction and looting. As a result, it provides a unique insight into the world of the Hungarian aristocracy in the 18C and 19C.

▶**Location:** Keszthely is 15km/7mi east of Hévíz. **By train:** there are direct connections between Keszthely Station (on Mártírok utca) and Tapolca, Zamárdi, Sümeg and Székesfehérvár. **By bus:** the bus station is next to the railway station. There are direct connections with Hévíz and Budapest *(for information and reservations see: volanbusz.hu/en).*

▶**Info: Tourist Office** – *Kossuth Lajos utca 30. ☎ 314 144. west-balaton.hu. Open summer, 9am–7pm (Sat & Sun, 4pm); check times for the rest of the year.*

▶**Tip:** This lovely little town is at the far western end of Lake Balaton. It is a good compromise for those yet to choose which shore they want to stay on, since both can be explored with ease from here.

Detachable map A6.

Ġ See *Addresses pp. 72 and 79*

FESTETICS-KASTÉLY★★

(Festetics Palace)
Helikon Kastélymúzeum. Kastély utca 1. ☎ 314 194. helikonkastely.hu. Open May, Jun & Sept, Mon–Sun, 10am–5pm; Jul & Aug,Mon–Sun, 9am–6pm (Wed, 9am–noon); Oct–Apr, Tue–Sun, 10am–5pm. Palace and coach museum, Ft2, 700; palace and all exhibitions, Ft3,900. Parking nearby (charges apply).

With around a hundred rooms, there is more than enough space for the **Helikon Palace Museum** that is housed here. If you detect a slight British feel to the place, you would be spot on, as the extensions that Duke Tasziló Festetics added between 1883 and 1887 were supervised by his wife, Mary, a Scottish duchess.

If you are short of time, don't leave without seeing the library. On your way, you will pass through up to 18 rooms, some reconstructed but most with their original interiors, including coffered ceilings, a majestic carved staircase, Rococo furniture, works of art and much more. They recreate the aristocratic lifestyle of the 18C and

Festetics Palace

19C. After the Second World War, an officer in the Soviet army saved the interiors by sealing up the entrances to protect the palace from looting.

Helikon Library★★ – Along with the library at Zirc Abbey (♿︎*see p. 57*), this is one of the most famous libraries in Hungary. It was founded in 1799 by **Count György Festetics** (1755–1819), an enlightened patron of the arts and versed in the sciences. He also created the Georgikon, Europe's first agricultural college. Hence among the library's 86,000 volumes are many works on agriculture and raising livestock. The library owes its name to the count's love of Greek literature. He organized the Helikon literary festival, inviting the most eminent writers of the day to the palace.

English Garden – Designed in the naturalistic style by English landscape artist Ernest Miller in 1889. It includes a Palm House, opened in 2012, and a small area with farm animals.

Coach Museum – *In the English Garden.* A fine collection of horse-drawn coaches, carriages and sleighs. Two other permanent exhibitions (**hunting**, **historic model railways**), can be found in the palace grounds.

THE TOWN

The main entrance to the palace is on Kastély utca.

Amazon Ház (Amazon House)– *Kastély utca 17. ℘ 314 194. Open Jul & Aug, Mon–Sun, 9am–6pm; May, Jun & Sept, Mon–Sun, 10am–5pm; Oct–Apr, Tue–Sun, 10am–5pm. Ft1,300. There's also a café on site.*
Filled with period artefacts (trunks,

travel irons, costumes...), the museum helps you to relive the Grand Tours of the aristocracy, which would eventually lead to tourism becoming fashionable for all, and to discover Lake Balaton's first tourists, too.
Follow Kossuth Lajos utca, a pleasant pedestrianized street.

Fő tér – The town hall (Polgármesteri Hivatal), in Fő tér, the main square, dates from the end of the 18C.

Magyarok Nagyasszonya templom (Church of Our Lady of Hungary) – This Gothic church is decorated with 14C and 15C frescoes. Count György Festetics is buried in the crypt.

Georgikon Majormúzeum – *Bercsényi Miklós utca 65–67. ℘ 311 563. elmenygazdasag.hu. Open summer, 9am–5pm (Wed, 8pm); check times for the rest of the year. Ft600.*
The Georgikon Institute, the agricultural college founded by György Festetics, was based here until 1848. The building became a museum in 1972 and traces the history of wine-growing and agriculture.

Balatoni Múzeum – *Múzeum utca 2. ℘ 312 351. balatonimuzeum.hu. Open 9am–5pm: June–Aug, daily; Apr, Oct & Nov, Mon–Fri; May & Sept, Mon–Sat. Ft900.* This neo-Baroque building (1928) houses a museum dedicated to Lake Balaton's geological and ethnographic history. A slideshow explores the Kis-Balaton (♿︎*see p. 33*).

Beaches – Helikon and Városi beaches are the most popular. An entry fee in summer (*8.30am–7pm, Ft800/400*), but the amenities are good and suitable for children. Városi has a swimming pool and waterslides. Wind- and kitesurfing boards for hire.

Veszprém★

This small picturesque university city lies in the Bakony Valley, with its historic centre and steep, cobbled streets concealed behind the walls of its castle, high up overlooking the Séd river below. Hungarians call it 'the city of queens' as it was here that the powerful bishops of Veszprém crowned the queens of Hungary. The city was almost completely destroyed by Turkish troops in the 17C, but it was rebuilt in the 18C, explaining much of the superb Baroque architecture you see today. The seat of the country's first bishopric has been well restored, turning former palaces into museums and galleries. This cultural wealth will be in the spotlight in 2023 when the town becomes the European Capital of Culture.

▶**Location:** Veszprém is 17km/10.5mi north of Lake Balaton, approaching from Balatonfüred. The historic centre lies within the old castle, while the modern centre spreads out around the nearby pedestrianized street, Kossuth Lajos utca. **By train:** there are around 20 trains a day from Budapest *(the fastest takes 1hr 25min)*. **By bus:** the bus station is near the train station (on Jutasi út 4). Frequent services to Sümeg, Keszthely and Siófok *(2hrs)*, Budapest *(2hrs 15min)* and Tapolca *(1hr)*.

▶**Info: Tourist Office** – *Óváros tér 2.* 📞 *404 548. veszpreminfo.hu.* A map in English and other leaflets. See: 2023veszprem.hu/en/ for information on Veszprém as the European Capital of Culture in 2023.
▶**Tip:** As the historic centre is concentrated along a single street inside the castle precinct, it can be explored on foot. Conveniently, right beside it, Óváros tér has plenty of parking places *(charges apply 7am–5pm,)*.
Detachable map E3.
♿ See *Addresses pp. 72 and 79.*

THE OLD TOWN★

Enter the Old Town beneath **Hősök Kapuja** (Heroes' Gate), but just before you go through, climb up **Tűztorony** (Fire Watchtower, *open 9am–5pm, Ft800*) for a superb **panorama**★★ over the city and its surroundings, including the forests of the Bakony Mountains.
ℹ Information panels in English are dotted around the castle precinct.

Vár utca
(Castle Street)
This winding, rather grand pedestrianized street begins at Heroes' Gate and is lined on either side with entranceways large enough to take carriages. Among the buildings of interest is no. 21, designed by Jakab Fellner, the Esterházy family's architect who also built the **Archbishop's Palace** at no. 16, considered one of the

City of queens

King István (Stephen) I, the first king of Hungary, founded the country's first bishopric and built the fortress in Veszprém in the 11C. His wife Gisela (who was beatified in 1911) was crowned in the fortress. All Hungary's queens were subsequently crowned here by the city's powerful archbishops and so Veszprém came to be known as the 'city of queens'. It was said to be Gisela's favourite city and many of the queens who followed her also became attached to it, making it a favourite royal residence.

masterpieces of Hungarian Baroque *(not open to the public)*. The whole street is a fine example of the Baroque style.

Modern Képtár★
(Gallery of Modern Art)

Vár utca 29. ℘ 561 310. vasscollection.hu. Open May–Oct, Mon–Sat, 10am–6pm; Nov–Apr, Mon–Sat, 10–5pm. Ft800.
Housing the László Vass Collection of modern art and design, this small museum comes as a pleasant surprise. It includes works by Bernar Venet, Gerrit Rietveld, Günther Uecker, Christo, silkscreen prints by Aurélie Nemours and nests of tables by Josef Albers, a key member of the Bauhaus.

Dubniczay palota★
(Dubniczay Palace)

Vár utca 29. ℘ 560 507. muveszetekhaza.hu/hu/vizit. Open May–Oct, Tue–Sun, 10am–6pm; Nov–Apr, Tue–Sun, 10am–5pm. Ft1,000.
Discover an interesting collection of **contemporary Hungarian art** (the Carl László Collection) displayed in the Baroque rooms of this beautiful renovated palace. It features the work of around 30 artists assembled in the 1980s. A modern, brick-built annexe (the Tegularium) in the garden houses

a collection of … 1,400 bricks! They were all made in Hungary and date from Roman times to the present day. Unfortunately, there is little information in English.

Salesianum

Vár utca 31. szalezianum.hu. Open June–Aug, daily, 9am–5pm; mid-Mar–May, Tue–Sun, 9am–5pm; Oct–mid-Mar, Tue–Sat, 9am–5pm. Ft1,200 (combined ticket including the cathedral Ft1,500).
A beautiful and well-restored palace that now houses the town's tourist centre. An exhibition celebrates one of its previous residents, **Bishop Márton Padányi Biró** (1693–1762), a powerful member of the Hungarian Church. Items of furniture and works of art from the period make this a very interesting visit, especially as the surroundings are so opulent. There is also a violin-maker's workshop on site and a small café, the only place inside the castle precinct where you can eat (✿see p. 79).

Szent Mihály Bazilika
(St. Michael's Cathedral Basilica)

Open beg May–mid Oct, Tue–Sun, 10am–5pm (closed Mon & during mass). Ft500 (combined ticket including the Salesianum Ft1,500).

Veszprém

Founded in the 11C, the cathedral has been destroyed and rebuilt several times, most recently in 1910. Only the **Romanesque crypt★** has survived from the original medieval building. This is where you may see some of the faithful prostrating themselves before a relic – a bone from the forearm of Queen Gisela (*see box p. 54*) – brought here in 1996 from Bavaria in Germany, the country of her birth. Several other remains can be seen close by, displayed under a transparent dome.

Gizella-kápolna★
(Gisela Chapel)
Vár str. 16. ℘ 426 095. veszpreminfo. hu/record/gisella-chapel. Open May–Oct, 10am–6pm. By appointment at other times.
Discovered in the 18C when work began on building the palace, this chapel is thought to date from the 13C, prompted by the Byzantine-inspired frescoes decorating the walls.

Gizella Királyné Múzeum
Vár utca 35. ℘ 426 095. Open 10am–5pm. Ft400.
Sacred objects from the bishopric treasury are displayed in this museum along with Christian works of art. **Szent István ferences templom** (Church of St. Stephen), which belongs to the Franciscan Order, stands next to the museum.
Vár utca ends at the city walls. Looking out at the view from here, you can see Benedek-hegy (St. Benedict Hill), one of the seven hills on which the city was traditionally founded, and as far

as the viaduct over the River Séd. The statues of Hungary's first royal couple, King Stephen and Queen Gisela, erected in 1938 on the 900th anniversary of Stephen's death, stand guard over the city here as well.

EXCURSIONS

Herendi Porcelánmanufaktúra★
(Herend Porcelain Factory)
D2 15km/9.3mi west of Veszprém by Rte 830. Kossuth Lajos u. 140. ℘ 261 518. herend.com. Open beg Apr–Oct, daily, 9.30am–6pm; Nov–Mar, Tue–Sat, 10am–4pm (closed 3rd wk Dec–3rd wk Feb). Minimanufactory, incl. guided tour in English & Porcelain Museum Ft3,500 (photography permit, Ft1,100).
Herend porcelain has been gracing the tables of the fashionable and the wealthy for close to 200 years. At the time the factory was built (in 1826), Japanese and Chinese porcelain could command prices on a level with gold, but thanks to their advanced production techniques, Herend's porcelain was well able to compete. Many of Europe's royal families, including Britain's Queen Victoria, ordered Herend dinner services. Nationalized in 1948, the factory was bought back by its workers in 1992. Today it is flourishing once more. Several brick buildings housing a Minimanufactory enclose a small square with an ornamental pond. This is where the porcelain-making process is demonstrated, while the Porcelain Museum showcases many of the most beautiful pieces. Your

visit ends by passing through the shop where lovely pieces are on sale, admittedly with prices to match.

Öskü kerektemplom
(Öskü Chapel)
F2 18km/11mi north-east of Veszprém by Rte 8.

Take a minor detour through the countryside to something of a curiosity, a large, quite unique and very old mushroom-shaped building, which overlooks the modest village of Öskü. It is one of the very few circular churches in Europe. Capped with a hemispherical roof, its walls date from the 11C, while the roof and the choir are 15C.

⊛ Opposite the church is a small park crossed by a stream with wooden tables and benches. If your visit happens to coincide with lunchtime, it's the perfect place for a picnic.

Zirci apátság★
(Zirc Abbey)
E1 25km/15.5mi north of Veszprém by Rte 82.

Zirc, a small town in the Bakony Mountains, is known for its Cistercian abbey (18C), an immense building that is at odds with the otherwise modest size of the old town centre (parking in adjacent streets, no charge).

Welcome Centre – ☎ 593 675. zirciapatsag.hu. Open Tue–Sun, 9am–5pm (Nov–Apr, 10am–4pm). Tours every hour. Library and church: visit by guided tour only (1hr); Ft800 each (combined ticket, Ft900). Visitor centre Ft1,000; arboretum Ft800; all-inclusive ticket Ft2,900.

You have to pass through the ticket office/shop to join the guided tours. The tours are in Hungarian, but there are English leaflets about the library.
Library★ – If pressed for time, make this your priority. Tucked away on the first floor of the main building, it is the abbey's masterpiece – the work of a local cabinetmaker (1857), its collection of 65,000 volumes are displayed on shelves of cherrywood. There is a wealth of material, including rare manuscripts, 70 incunabla (books printed prior to 1501), a Bible in nine languages. Also one of the oldest celestial globes (1630).

On your way out, visit the very ornate **abbey church**, decorated with frescoes by the Austrian artist Franz-Anton Maulbertsch (1724–96) above the high altar and the south altar. Finally, an **arboretum**, planted with rare species, extends for nearly 20ha/50 acres behind the abbey.

Kékfestő Múzeum, Pápa★★
(Blue Dye Fabric Museum)
C1 50km/31mi north-west of Veszprém (45km/28mi west of Zirc). Március 15. tér 12. ☎ (89) 324 390. kekfestomuzeum.hu. Open Apr–Oct, Tue–Sun, 9am–5pm; Nov–Mar, Tue–Sat, 10am–4pm. Ft900.

Visit the historic town of Pápa to see the former kékfestő (blue dyed fabric) factory, preserved in its original state with all its equipment and now a museum. The only things missing are the workers and the fabrics dripping with dye. You can also see an exhibition of blue-dye fabrics by 20C artist Irén Bódy (1925–2011).

Székesfehérvár★★

*Seen from the highway linking Budapest with Lake Balaton,
you may feel inclined to pass Székesfehérvár by, put off by the industrial
districts and blocks of high-rise flats that seem to dominate the horizon. But
to do so would be a mistake. The Baroque centre of its old town is dotted with
lovely churches, museums and pretty little streets lined with café terraces. And
for Hungarians, Székesfehérvár is almost sacred, the place where kings were
crowned for five centuries and where Stephen I, the first and most famous
of them all, is buried. He is also known as St. Stephen, or sometimes King St.
Stephen (Szent István király), as he was canonized by Pope Gregory VII in 1083.
Many visitors miss out on this city's riches. Don't join them!*

▶**Location:** Székesfehérvár is halfway between Budapest and Balatonfüred. The
city centre occupies a roughly triangular-shaped area between Mátyás Király
körút to the west, Várkörút to the east and Budai utca to the south. **By train:** the
railway station is 2km/1.2mi south-east of Városház tér on Béke tér. There are
connections with Budapest *(1hr)*, Balatonfüred *(1hr 2min)* and Siófok *(34 min)*.
By bus: pretty much the same destinations as by train, but with the advantage
that the bus station is nearer the centre *(on Piac tér 4–8)*.
▶**Info: Tourist Office** – Oskola utca 2–4. ℘ *(23) 537 261. turizmus.szekesfehervar.
hu. Open Jul–Aug, daily, 9am–6pm; Sat & Sun, 10am–4pm; check times for the
rest of the year.* The staff are very efficient and there is free Wifi along with
plenty of maps and brochures.
Detachable map GH2.
♿ *See* Addresses *pp. 72, 79 and 87.*

THE OLD TOWN

Start the visit on Városház tér.
The town hall (Polgármesteri Hivatal)
is on this pleasant square surrounded
by café terraces and facing the
Franciscan church. The Bishop's
Palace (Püspöki Palota) was built in
the Zopf (late-Baroque) style at the
beginning of the 19C, using stones
from the royal palace and the remains
of the medieval basilica.
*Take Koronázó tér to reach the
Medieval Ruin Garden.*

Középkori Romkert★
(National Memorial/Medieval Ruin Garden)
℘ *317 572. szikm.hu/kiallitohelyek/
nemzeti_emlekhely. Open 9am–5pm.
Ft700.*
This site is an important part of
Hungarian history as it contains the
remains of the basilica founded by
Stephen I (circa 975–1038). In all, 37
kings of Hungary were crowned and
some 20 are buried here, including
Stephen I himself, who lies in the
white marble sarcophagus at the

Town Hall Square with the Orb and the Bishop's Palace

entrance. The basilica was destroyed in 1601 after gunpowder being stored nearby exploded.
Return to Városház tér and turn left down Kossuth utca.

Kossuth utca★

This is a lively street with intriguing interior courtyards and passageways leading off. It manages to seamlessly integrate modern architecture in a period setting. At the junction with Táncsics Mihály utca, you will see **Árpád Fürdő** (baths, *p. 87*) and next door a pink building in the Secessionist style.
Turn right towards Arany János utca.

Szent István székesegyház
(St. Stephen's Cathedral)
Closed for renovation work until 2022.
The cathedral was built in the 18C on the site of a 13C church where King Béla IV was crowned in 1235. The Baroque building you see today is the work of Austrian court architect Franz Anton Hildebrandt. Austrian artist Johann Cimbal painted the ceiling frescoes. **King Béla III** and his wife Agnes of Antioch lie at rest in the crypt. Outside, on the north wall, the Christ on the Cross is dedicated to the victims of the Hungarian Uprising in 1956.

Szent Anna kápolna
(St. Anne's Chapel)
The only building from the medieval period (1470) to survive, this small, modest chapel stands facing the cathedral. Inside is a lovely Baroque altar dating from the 18C.
Walk down Arany János utca.

Szent István tér
An equestrian statue of **King St. Stephen** stands in the centre of this pleasant square (after whom it is named). There are several benches if you'd like to pause here for a rest.
To return to Városház tér, walk back up **Megyehaz utca** looking out for the two neo-Romanesque buildings at nos. 7 and 11, dating from the late 18C.

60

A royal city

After Esztergom, Székesfehérvár was the most important city in the Kingdom of Hungary. István (Stephen) I was crowned here and chose it as the location for his palace and the place where the crown jewels and the kingdom's archives would be stored.

It was also on a hill near Székesfehérvár that King András II attached his seal to the Golden Bull he issued in 1222. Sometimes considered the first Hungarian Constitution, it recognized the right of the barons to rebel against their king without being punished for treason if the sovereign abused his power.

Many kings were crowned and buried in the city after Stephen, including Louis II in 1526. He died fighting the Turkish invaders at the Battle of Mohács. Székesfehérvár fell into the hands of the Turks in 1543. They left it in ruins and its reconstruction was not completed until the end of the 18C. Later, the railway contributed to the city's development. After the Second World War, industry in the form of aluminium smelting and the manufacture of buses and TVs drew in more people, resulting in the residential blocks you see today.

*Cross Városház tér and continue on
Oskola utca.*

Deák Gyűjtemény★
(Deák Collection)
*Oskola utca 10. ℘ 329 431.
deakgyujtemeny.hu. Open Tue–Sun,
10am–6pm. Ft700.*
If you only have time to visit one
of the city's museums, make it this
one. A rich and interesting collection
of **Hungarian paintings** from the
1900s to the 1960s is housed in a
gorgeous 18C building. The 600 or
so works were assembled by the
collector Dénes Deák (1931–93), who
bequeathed them to the city, along
with a number of sculptures (in the
basement).
*Return to the pedestrianized main
street, Fő utca.*

Fekete Sas Patikamúzeum★
(Black Eagle Pharmacy)
*Fő utca 5. ℘ 315 583. Open Tue–Sun,
10am–6pm. Ft700.* A 300-year-old
pharmacy, which only closed in 1971.
Its beautiful carved wooden shop
fittings were installed in the 18C. On
its shelves you can see old bottles,
jars and instruments used by the
pharmacists of days gone by.

Szent János Nepomuk templom★
(St. John of Nepomuk Church)
Built by the Jesuits (1745–51), this
church was subsequently taken over
by the Cistercians. Frescoes cover
the walls and ceiling inside. Look out
for the gilded wooden pulpit dating
from the 18C. In the **sacristy** you can
see wooden furniture (oak and lime),
carved in the Rococo style by a Jesuit
priest and a perfect fit for the room.

Szent István Király Múzeum★★
*Országzászló tér 3. ℘ 315 583. szikm.
hu. Closed for work.*
The ground floor of this museum
displays a collection of stones and
sculptures from Roman times, the
most significant of which came from
the Roman city of Gorsium (&see
p. 62). The upper floor is dedicated
to the archaeological history of the
region from prehistory to the end of
the Turkish occupation.

BEYOND THE OLD TOWN

Rácváros
(Old Serbian Quarter)
*Take Ady Endre utca and then its
continuation (Tobak utca) to Rác utca.*
In the 16C, during the Ottoman
occupation, this part of the town was
settled by Serbs. Rác utca (Serbian
Street) is a reminder of this period,
with a row of a dozen or so houses
with thatched roofs that have been
restored to form a small open-air
museum (**Palotavárosi Skanzen**;
℘ 315 583; open May–Oct, Mon–Fri,
9am–5pm; Ft700). It traces the
history of the area and its merchants
and craftsmen. The **Rác templom** (a
single-nave church) contains a very
beautiful **iconostasis★★** (a screen
covered with icons and religious
paintings) from the 18C.

Bory vár★
(Bory Castle)
*Head north from the centre, take
Szekfü Gyula. Cross the junction onto
Berény út. Continue straight ahead,
crossing the road onto Béla út. Turn
right after the cemetery into Bicskei*

61

utca, then take Máriavölgy utca to reach Bory tér. bory-var.hu/en. Open daily 9am–5pm. Ft1,800.

A strange but amazing building in a mix of different styles created by **Jenő Bory** (1879–1959), an architect and sculptor who was born in Székesfehérvár. He spent some 40 years building this astonishing structure with his own hands.

EXCURSIONS

Gorsium Régészeti Park★, Tác
(Gorsium Archaeological Park)

H3 15km/9.5mi south of Székesfehérvár by highway M7 (exit 70). ℘ 315 583. szikm.hu/ kiallitohelyek/gorsium. Open Tue– Sun: Apr–Oct, 10am–6pm; Nov–Mar, 8am–4pm. Ft1,200. A large car park on site.

The remains of the Roman city of Gorsium-Herculia lie around 2km/1.2mi from the village of Tác. A modern concrete building houses the museum which traces (in Hungarian) the history of this Roman city, which once had up to 7,000 inhabitants before it was destroyed by the barbarians in 260. The remains of the excavated city are quite extensive and include a street of shops, the governor's palace and two basilicas. A **theatre** capable of seating 1,200 spectators can be found at the edge of the site. After the Romans left, Gorsium was abandoned and the stones were reused to build houses in the surrounding area, notably at Székesfehérvár.

Velencei-tó★
(Lake Velence)

H2 10km/6mi east of Székesfehérvár by Rte 7.

🚩 Tópart u. 47, in Velence village. ℘ (30) 974 2566. velenceturizmus.hu.
👫 A mini Lake Balaton and less well known to foreign visitors, Lake Velence covers an area of 26sq km/10sq mi. Covered with reedbeds, it is a nature reserve that is popular with environmentalists and ornithologists. The southern shore has been developed as a resort area for holidaymakers. The shallow water and grass beaches make it an attractive place for families, although the choice of accommodation and restaurants is a bit limited.

Károlyi-kastély★
(Károly Castle)

G1 At Fehérvárcsurgó, 19km/12mi east of Székesfehérvár by Rte 81.
Petőfi Sándor utca 2. ℘ (21) 311 0422. Visit by guided tour only (1hr), in English and Hungarian. Open 10am–5pm. Ft1,500.

The large and very grand Károly Castle seems to have landed as if by magic in the centre of the small village of Fehérvárcsurgó. Renovated by the Franco-Hungarian descendants of one of Hungary's aristocratic families, it is worth seeing today more for its elegant French-style grounds than for its interior, which has been badly damaged over the years. The castle was confiscated at the end of World War II, but the family managed to retrieve ownership and renovate it. Today it operates mainly as a hotel-restaurant (see p. 73).

62

Addresses

65

Find our addresses in the Michelin Guide: Main Cities of Europe *by scanning the QR code here.*

Terrace of Laposa Birtok, Badacsony
© Reinhard Schmid/Sime/Photononstop

🍴

Where to eat

In Budapest, as in the towns and villages of the Lake Balaton region, most restaurants have a reasonably priced set menu for lunch (*mai menü*), along with à la carte options.

♿ Find the address on our maps using the number in the listing (❶). The coordinates in red (C2) will help you to find it easily on the detachable map (inside the cover).

BUDAPEST
Detachable map

😊There are many unpretentious but good restaurants in the **Belváros** district, on Ráday utca (Ⓜ 3 or 4 Kálvin tér). Around **Andrássy út**, on Liszt Ferenc tér (Ⓜ 1 Oktogon), restaurants stay open until very late in the evening. Those in the **Erzsébetváros** district, on Dob utca (Ⓜ 1, 2 or 3 Deák Ferenc tér) are also a good option.

VÁRNEGYED (CASTLE DISTRICT)

Ft10,000–20,000
❶ 21 – *B4* – *Fortuna utca 21.* Ⓜ *4 Széll Kálmán tér.* ✆ *(1) 202 2113. 21restaurant.hu. Open noon–11.45pm. Ft8,800/12,000.*
Enjoy dining outside on the terrace during the day and inside in the friendly bistro atmosphere during the evening. The chef fuses traditional Hungarian cuisine with contemporary flavours, while avoiding the usual Hungarian restaurant clichés.

VÍZIVÁROS

Ft5,000–10,000
❷ **Csalogány26.** - *B3* –*Csalogány utca 26.* Ⓜ *2 Batthyány tér or Széll Kálmán tér.* ✆ *(1)201 7892. csalogany26.hu. Open Tue–Wed, noon–3pm; Thu–Sat, noon–3pm & 7pm–10pm. 3-course lunch menu Ft3,100. Tasting menu: 5 courses Ft15,000, with wine Ft20,000. Or à la carte for dinner.*
A small but popular restaurant 5 mins walk from the Castle District. The food is carefully prepared and cooked using fresh seasonal ingredients, served in a modern interior and is good value, particularly the fixed price lunch.

BELVÁROS

Ft5,000–10,000
❸ **Károlyi Étterem és Kávéház** – *E6 Károlyi Mihály utca 16.* Ⓜ *2 Astoria.* ✆ *(1) 328 0240. www.karolyietterem. hu. Open noon–11pm. Ft7,500/11,100.*
This restaurant enjoys a charming and historic setting within the courtyard of the town house of the counts of Károly, which is shaded by huge trees and lined with elegant buildings. The menu is essentially Hungarian (fish soup, goulash, stuffed cabbage), but includes European culinary touches and also caters for diners with food allergies (ask for details). A pianist generally plays from 7pm.

Marvel Tour Budapest

🍴

4 **Múzeum Kávéház és Étterem** – *E6*
Múzeum körút 12. Ⓜ *2 Astoria.*
✆ *(1) 338 4221. muzeumkavehaz.hu.*
Open Tue–Sat, 6pm–midnight. Closed
public holidays. Ft8,400/12,900.
Fans of traditional Hungarian
cooking will enjoy this venue, which
has been open since 1885 (pike-perch
fillet à la Múzeum, trout, Hortobágy
pancakes). A Belle Epoque interior
with faïence tiles, wood detailing and
high ceilings.

ANDRÁSSY ÚT

Ft5,000-10,000

5 **Két Szerecsen** – *E4* – *Nagymező*
utca 14. Ⓜ *1 Opera.* ✆ *(1) 343 1984.*
ketszerecsen.hu. Open 8am–midnight
(Sat & Sun, 9am–midnight).
Ft7,400/11,500. Boasting a central
location and a pleasant bistro
atmosphere, this place is popular with
the locals. Don't expect fine dining
but its soups, salads and Hungarian
dishes with a French twist should hit
the spot. A terrace in summer.

VÁROSLIGET

Ft10,000–20,000

6 **Robinson** – *G1* – *Városligeti tó.*
Ⓜ *1 Széchenyi Fürdő.* ✆ *(30) 663 6871.*
www.robinsonrestaurant.hu. Open
lunch noon–4pm, dinner 6pm–11pm.
Ft11,023/14,589. Situated right by
the water in Városliget (City Park),
Robinson is on two levels in a lovely
location, with a substantial terrace.
This is an award-winning restaurant
serving Hungarian and Mediterranean
cuisine, with a steakhouse upstairs.

ERZSÉBETVÁROS

Under Ft5,000

7 **Kazimir** – *E5* – *Kazinczy utca 34.*
Ⓜ *1, 2 or 3 Deák Ferenc tér.*
✆ *(20) 354 5533.* ✆ *(1) 798 5747.*
bistro.kazimir.hu. Open 10am–
midnight; Thu–Sat, 10am–2am. Menu
Ft1,490. Opposite the Orthodox
synagogue in the Old Jewish Quarter,
the emphasis in this restaurant is
on tradition. A warm welcome and
free jazz concerts at 9pm on some
evenings.

Ft5,000-10,000

8 **Mazel Tov** – *E4–5* – *Akácfa*
utca 47. 🚋 *4, 6 Erzsébet körút.*
✆ *(70) 626 4280. mazeltov.hu. Open*
Sun–Wed 11am–1am (Thu–Sat, 2am).
Ft5,270/6,730. Delicious Israeli street
food (a shawarma sandwich) or
something more elaborate (lamb with
grilled aubergine) is served in a lovely
atrium. A jazz group plays in the
evening and during Sunday brunch.
Reservation necessary to avoid dining
in the less appealing adjacent room.

LAKE BALATON
Detachable map

◉ The free publications *We Love*
Balaton and *Funzine* (🕭*see p.106*)
feature recommendations in English.
Free maps of food venues and wine
routes are available from the local
tourist offices. Many Hungarians are
also happy to chat and share their
restaurant recommendations with
visitors. Places do change hands quite
often in the area, so locals are a good
source of information on the latest
eateries to try.

AROUND THE LAKE (NORTH SHORE)

Under Ft3,500

🅐 **⑨ Sáfránkert Vendéglő – *E4* –** *Fő utca 1, Paloznak. ☏ (70) 624 4448. homolapinceszet.hu/safrankert-vendeglo. Open Thu–Sun, noon–9.30pm. Ft2,290/4,290.* Situated between Balatonalmádi and Balatonfüred. Take a small detour to find the charming village of Paloznak, where a vineyard has opened this small bistro and wine bar. The decor is simple and the concise menu on the blackboard focuses on local seasonal produce and house wines. Hungarian cuisine with a contemporary feel.

🅐 **⑬ Neked Főztem Gasztrokocsma – *D5* –** *Fő utca 7, Zánka. ☏ (70) 365 1003. restu.hu/neked-foztem. Open summer, noon–9pm. Ft2,950/4,290.* Situated between Tihany and Badacsony, this small country restaurant serves dishes that transcend their Hungarian roots via modern culinary techniques, delivering refined and delicious dishes. The large and splendid terrace is overlooked by the church tower and the service is very good. It is often full so it's best to reserve a table

Ft3,500–7,000

🅐 **⑩ Bisztró Szent Donát – *E4* –** *Szitahegyi utca 28, Csopak. ☏ (20) 928 1181. szentdonat.hu. Open Oct–May, Thu–Mon, noon–9pm. Ft3,990/4,990.* Situated just east of Balatonfüred, this elegant venue opened in 2014 on the family wine estate of the same name. It boasts a good menu and a terrace with a panoramic view of the vines and lake.

⑪ Bakos Attila Vendéglője – *B6* – *Iharos utca 4, Szigliget. ☏ (87) 461210. bakosvendeglo.hu. Open Wed–Sun, noon–9pm. Ft2,950/4,250.* A feast for the eyes as well as the stomach in this restaurant that is full, floor to ceiling, with paintings, photos and religious objects. Good rustic cuisine served on check tablecloths. Try the delicious Hoffman carp stew and other lake fish specialities. A large terrace.

⑫ Szászi Birtok – *B6* – *Hegymagas, Mókus krt, Szigliget. ☏ (30) 690 8808. szaszibirtok.hu. Open daily in summer, check times for rest of the year. Ft3,200/5,500.* Szászi Birtok lies in the heart of the vineyards. The terrace and dining room of this bistro open onto the estate vineyard. It is in a great setting and serves elegant food with wine pairings.

AROUND THE LAKE (SOUTH SHORE)

Under Ft3,500

⑭ Paprika Csárda – *E5* – *Honvéd utca 1, Zamárdi. ☏ (84) 348 705. www.paprikacsarda.eu/en. Open 10am–10pm (Fri & Sat 11pm). Ft2,450/4,950.* Open year-round (unlike most places on the south shore), this large restaurant in the neighbouring district to Siófok is housed in a traditional building with a shaded patio and has been in business for over 50 years. The menu features an impressive number of specialities, from fried foie gras

🍴

to catfish. The simpler the dish, the better in this case.

⑯ Rozmaring Kiskert Vendéglő és Pizzéria – *E5* – *Akácfa utca 53. Siófok. ℘ (30) 694 0949. Open Wed–Sun, noon–9pm. Ft1,290/3,990.* The locals love this Italian restaurant, which serves the best Neapolitan pizza ... in Lake Balaton! Grilled meat dishes and pasta also available. A concise menu with delicious choices that will appeal to food lovers. Reservation recommended.

Ft3,500–7,000

⑮ Kistücsök Étterem – *D6* – *Bajcsy Zs. utca 25, Balatonszemes. ℘ (84) 360 133. kistucsok.hu. Open noon–10pm. Menu (5 dishes) Ft9,900. À la carte Ft3,490/4,990.* It should come

as no surprise that this restaurant features frequently on the lists of the best restaurants in Lake Balaton. Both owner, Balázs Csapody, and restaurant have enjoyed continued success thanks to chef László Jahni, who has been in charge since he was in his twenties. Good value from a Western European point of view. appeal to food lovers. Reservation recommended.

BALATONFÜRED

Under Ft3,500

⑰ Kredenc Borbisztró – *E4* – *Blaha Lujza utca 7. ℘ (20) 518 9960. kredencborbisztro.hu. Open summer, noon–10pm (Sat & Sun 11.30pm);*

© Tajti Krisztián/orokkep.net/Szászi Birtok

Szászi Birtok, Hegymagas

check times for the rest of the year. *Ft1,990/2,990.* A good spot in which to discover vintage wines. This atmospheric wine bar is centrally located with a pavement terrace. Concerts some evenings.

Ft3,500–7,000

🙂 **18** **Baricska Csárda** – *E4* – *Baricska dűlő. ☎ (070) 621 9944. baricska.hu. Open daily 11.30am–10.30pm. Ft2,690/7,390.* It might be a touch touristy (it is a short walk from the marina and promenade), but this elegant traditional tavern next to a vineyard is still a charming spot. It has a lovely terrace shaded by vines and with views of the lake and Tihany Peninsula. The cuisine is classic Hungarian accompanied by wines from the local area and beyond. Romani musicians add to the atmosphere *(Fri & Sat pm, Sunday lunch).*

TIHANY

Under Ft3,500

19 **Apáti Étterem és Kávézó** – *E5* – *Romkápolna utca 2, at Sajkod. ☎ (30) 566 7356. apatietterem.hu. Open Fri–Sun, 11am–9pm. Ft1,850/3,990.* In a green and secluded area at the foot of the Tihany Peninsula, this place attracts foodies from around Hungary with its pizzas. It also serves a delicious foie gras. A nice terrace beneath an awning and play equipment for the children.

Ft3,500–7,000

🙂 **20** **Gulyás Udvar Étterem** – *E5* – *Mádl Ferenc tér 2. ☎ 438 051. gulyasudvar.hu. Open summer, 11am–10pm; check times for the rest of the year. Ft2,800/4,400.* Take a seat in this traditional tavern near the bottom of the steps that lead up to the abbey and select from the comprehensive menu: goulash, braised pork with cabbage, fried carp and strudel are all included. Food is grilled on the barbecue on the terrace in the evenings.

BADACSONY

Ft3,500–7,000

21 **Muskátli Étterem** – *C6* – *Balaton utca 2, Badacsonytomaj. ☎ (87) 471 167. muskatli-vendeglo.hu. Open 9am–8pm. Ft2,090/4,890.* A small traditional village tavern offering honest and hearty family cuisine: tripe stew, fried foie gras, *galuska* (a pasta dish). A good local address, open year-round.

22 **Kővirág** – *C5* – *Fő utca 9/A. 8274 Köveskál (Káli Basin). ☎ (70) 418 7713. kovirag.hu. Open summer, noon– 10pm; check times for rest of the year. Ft3,200/6,700. Also has 6 rooms for accommodation from Ft19,000 ☜.* This is an innovative place (restaurant plus rooms) that highlights the way that food and tourism are being revitalized in the area. The rooms, like the food, are charming and modern and yet have traditional flourishes. They use regional produce and their signature dishes include Kővirág

cottage cheese dumplings. The
menu changes every three days and
vegetarian options are available. It's a
great place.

HÉVÍZ

Ft3,500–7,000
23 **Öreg Harang Borozó** – *A6* –
*Zrínyi utca 181 (2.4km/1.5mi north of
Hévíz thermal lake). ℘ (30) 927 9011.
oregharang.hu. Open 3pm–10pm.
Ft2,390/5,690.* In a lovely setting
among the estate vines, the warm,
cozy atmosphere of this country
inn is echoed in its simple but good
Hungarian specialities, made using
regional ingredients. Diners sit on
rustic wooden benches or chairs and
often end their meals with the clinking
of glasses of *pálinka*.

KESZTHELY

Under Ft3,500
24 **Jóbarát Vendéglő** – *A6* –
*Martinovics utca 1 (2km/1.25mi east
of Festetics Palace). ℘ 311 422.
jobaratvendeglo.hu. Open 11am–10pm.
Ft1,990/3,500.* Recommended by
the locals, this inn with a simple
rustic charm is slightly out of the
way. There's a ceramic stove in the
center of the restaurant, which serves
house specialities that include a kind
of Hungarian gnocchi (*dödölle*) and
potato pancakes (*tócsni*). Jóbarát,
incidentally, means 'good friend'.

VESZPRÉM

Under Ft3,500
25 **Marica Kávéház** – *E3* – *Kossuth
Lajos utca 5. ℘ (70) 634 2403.
Open 10am–10pm (Fri & Sat, 1am).
Ft1,490–2,990.* Located on a
pedestrianized street in the modern
centre (just a few minutes' walk from
the castle), this small, unpretentious
café-restaurant is very popular with
students. It serves contemporary food
including burgers, pizzas and salads.
There is some delicious homemade
lemonade, too.
26 **Fricska Étteremlakás** – *E3* –
*Miklós utca 10. ℘ 794 331. Open
10am–11pm (Fri & Sat, 1 am). Ft1,290–
2,200.* Situated amid the greenery
in a beautiful garden alongside the
River Séd, near the foot of the hill
on which the castle stands, this
restaurant is worth the slight detour.
The atmosphere is a mix of beer
garden and open-air bistro and the
menu is based on grilled meat dishes
and burgers. Warm, welcoming, and
unpretentious.

SZÉKESFEHÉRVÁR

Under Ft3,500
27 **Rosetta Étterem** – *G2* – *Szent
István tér 14. ℘ 806 008. rosetta.hu.
Open 11.30am–10pm (Fri & Sat,
midnight). Ft1,000/2,000.* Located
at the junction of two streets and
overlooking a pretty square with
trees, this restaurant has a large
terrace and a feel of *la dolce vita* …
both in the air and on the plate.

© Dreana/Shutterstock

73

Károlyi-kastély, Fehérvárcsurgó

28 Perte Bistro – *G2* – *Lakatos utca 2. ☎ (70) 331 7831. Open 8am–10pm. Ft1,000/3,000.* On sunny days the large terrace, with a view of Városház tér, is very inviting. The contemporary interior is just as welcoming. Hearty food and delicious homemade drinks (lemonade, smoothies...).

Ft3,500–7,000

30 Károlyi-kastély – *G1* – *Petőfi Sándor utca 2; at Fehérvárcsurgó, 19km/12mi east of Székesfehérvár on Rte 81. ☎ (21) 311 0422. karolyikastely. hu. Ft2,550/5,650. Also 22 rooms for accommodation, Ft24,300* 🛏. This very grand building, owned by aristocrats during the days of the Austro-Hungarian Empire, houses a restaurant that promotes Franco-Hungarian entente cordiale on a daily basis in its dishes. It is also a hotel now owned by descendants of the original Franco-Hungarian owners.

Ft7,000–10,000

29 67Sigma Étterem – *G2* – *Oskola utca 2–4. ☎ (20) 970 4997. 67sigma.hu. Open 11.30am–10pm (Sat, 11pm). Closed Sun. Ft4,000/9,800.* In a Baroque building in the historic heart of town, with a newly decorated interior, this elegant restaurant is popular with local food lovers who enjoy the way the precision of the cooking and the perfectly balanced flavours result in excellent and tasty Hungarian dishes.

Where to drink

One of the great pleasures that awaits you on your visit to Hungary is the social life that revolves around its pavement cafés, tea rooms and bars. People go to chat and catch up on news or to relax and enjoy a little 'me time' with a good book. Whatever your preference, there's a wide choice of venues, from a leisurely pot of tea and mouth-watering pastry in a **cukrászda** (patisserie/tea room) or a homemade lemonade in a turn-of-the-century café, to a glass of delicious local wine on a terrace overlooking the vineyards.

🍸 Find the address on our maps using the number in the listing (❶). The coordinates in red (C2) will help you to find it easily on the detachable map (inside the cover).

BUDAPEST
Detachable map

VÁRNEGYED (CASTLE DISTRICT)

Tea room
❶ **Ruszwurm Cukrászda** – *B4* – *Szentháromság utca 7.* 📞 *(1) 375 5284. ruszwurm.hu. Open 10am–6pm.* With a Biedermeier-style interior and *krémes* (a sort of vanilla slice) on the menu, this is one of the oldest (and busiest) tea rooms in Hungary, patronized by royalty – Sissi (aka Empress Elisabeth of Austria) used to come here. Locals and tourists alike wait patiently for a table in the charming small salon whose boudoir-like interior has remained unchanged since 1827. Nostalgia for the past and pastry – the perfect combination.

GELLÉRTHEGY (GELLÉRT HILL)

Bar
❷ **Raqpart** – *D5* – *Jane Haining Rkp.* Ⓜ *1 Vörösmarty tér,* 🚊 *2 Eötvös tér.* 📞 *(30) 732 4751. raqpart.hu. Open June–Sept, noon–1am, Fri & Sat, noon–3am.* Situated beside the Danube and right by the Chain Bridge, this contemporary bar (only open in summer) is one of the best locations in which to enjoy a glass of something chilled while watching the sun set over the castle and the river. Electro sounds and wooden decking decor. Also serves lunch and dinner.

VÍZIVÁROS

Tea room
❸ **Angelika Kávéház** – *C3* – *Batthyány tér 7.* Ⓜ *2 Batthyány tér,* 🚊 *19, 41 Batthyány tér.* 📞 *(1) 225 1653. angelikacafe.hu. Open 9am–11pm (summer, midnight). Closed 24 Dec.* This tea room is on the riverfront, with a terrace overlooking the Parliament Building for sunny days and an attractive interior for less sunny ones. A wide range of pastries is on offer, including its house speciality, Angelika torta, a sort of sponge cake with chocolate and vanilla.

ERZSÉBETVÁROS

Tea room

😊 **④ Fröhlich Kóser Cukrászda – *E5***
Dob utca 22. Ⓜ *2 Astoria or Blaha Lujza tér.* ☎ *(1) 266 1733. frohlich.hu. Open 9am–6pm (Fri, 9am–2pm; Sun, 10am–6pm). Closed Sat.* Known for its Jewish pastries, this small Ashkenazi Jewish café and bakery is reputed by those in the know to serve the best *flódni* in town, an apple cake with nuts and poppy seeds. A family atmosphere, a warm welcome and the perfect spot for a snack, light meal or breakfast.

⑤ New York Café – *F5* *– Erzsébet krt 9–11.* Ⓜ *2 Blaha Lujza tér,* 🚊 *4, 6 Wesselényi utca.* ☎ *(1) 886 6167. newyorkcafe.hu. Open 8am–midnight.* Don't miss this legendary café. A family-friendly brunch menu (buffet until 11am) is free for children under 8 and is served downstairs. Afternoon tea for two is rather more expensive at Ft19,500.

LAKE BALATON
Detachable map

😊 Lake Balaton has some great open-air venues in which to enjoy a glass of wine lakeside or among the vines in the summer. There are plenty of options on the north shore, where they have long been an institution, and some of the most attractive are perched high up with splendid views. You can taste the estate wines, often accompanied by a plate of cheese or cold meats. They are open during good weather, usually from around 11am to 7pm (later at the weekend).

😊 If travelling by car: Hungary operates a zero tolerance policy towards drink-driving. In other words, designated drivers are advised to abstain and wait until someone else takes their turn at the wheel.

AROUND THE LAKE (NORTH SHORE)

Beach bar

⑥ BÁRmikor – *E4* *– István sétány 4–6, Balatonalmádi.* ☎ *(30) 263 79 49.* Quite literally the 'whenever you want' bar, this open-air venue is right by the water, and popular with local hipsters who appreciate its upcycled furniture, huge terrace and *fröccs* (wine spritzer), plus tapas for snacking while sipping your beverage of choice.

Vineyard wine terrace/bar

⑩ Homola Borterasz – *E4* *– Vincellér utca, Paloznak.* ☎ *(70) 431 2050.* Young locals love this open-air spot among the vines, where DJ evenings compete with quiet afternoons spent relaxing on the shaded terrace of the estate or on deckchairs with views of the lake in the distance.

⑪ Murci (Bencze Családi Birtok) *B6* *– Szent György-hegy, at Hegymagas (Szigliget).* ☎ *(30) 212 72 88. murci.hu.* Well known among the locals, Bencze Családi opened Hungary's first natural wine bar (only minimal chemical intervention is involved in the wine-making process). Among the vines on Szent György-hegy (hill), naturally.

Tea room

15 **G & D Kézműves Cukrászda és Pékség** – *F3* – *Fő utca 25, Balatonkenese.* 🕾 *(30) 203 6286.* This patisserie-tea room recently won the award for the best croissant in Hungary. Pastries, ice cream and sourdough bread are also on offer.

Ice cream shop

😊 😊 **16** **Vár Kávézó** – *B6* – *Kisfaludy utca 26, Szigliget.* 🕾 *(30) 622 2094.* Near the path leading up to the castle, this is a must for ice cream lovers. Choose from among the delicious homemade flavours at this award-winning but unassuming café. The pistachio ice cream has won a raft of prizes and the cakes are also delicious.

AROUND THE LAKE (SOUTH SHORE)

Beach venue

8 **A Konyhám** – *C7* – *Balatonpart utca 8, Balatonfenyves.* 🕾 *(20) 669 7894. Summer, 9am–midnight.* A small pretty café-restaurant with seating on decking right by the main beach, run by a former chef from Budapest. Brunch, salads, pancakes and waffles are all on the menu.

9 **Tiki Beach Bisztró** – *E5* – *Margó Ede sétány, Zamárdi.* 🕾 *(70) 678 0302. Summer, 10am–10pm.* A shaded terrace with seating on decking beside an area of grass. Close to the lake and the public beach, it is run by a young couple and classic snacks are on offer: burgers, salads and pizzas. Everything is extremely fresh.

Vineyard wine terrace/bar

12 **Kristinus Borbirtok** – *B8* – *Hunyadi utca 99, Kéthely.* 🕾 *(85) 539 014. kristinus.hu.* With both a restaurant and a hotel on site (👉*see p. 89*), the Kristinus Wine Estate also has its own alfresco wine-tasting venue on a shaded wooden platform with a lovely view of the vineyard. But if you'd prefer views of the lake, you can climb the neighbouring hill.

Ice cream shop

13 **Árkád Fagyizó** – *C6* – *Dózsa György utca 37, Balatonboglár.* An ice cream shop with a retro feel, it proves that Hungary's love affair with ice cream is here to stay and has become another intrinsic feature of the local lifestyle. Strawberry or pistachio? Cone or tub?

14 **La Rosa Fagyizó** – *F5* – *Batthyány Lajos utca 52, Siófok.* Floral flavours are the speciality here: rose, elderberry, lime.... But lovers of more traditional tastes have no need to worry, all the usual suspects are on offer, too (chocolate, vanilla, pistachio...) and are excellent.

BALATONFÜRED

Tea room

17 **Karolina** – *E4* – *Zákonyi Ferenc utca 4.* 🕾 *583 098. karolina.hu. Summer, 8am–midnight; check times for rest of the year.* Locals and tourists flock to this large tea room run by three brothers, lured by its large terrace and delicious cakes. Concerts are often also on offer at the weekend.

Café-restaurant

18 Vitorlás Étterem – *E4* – *Tagore sétány 1. ☎ (30) 546 0940. vitorlasetterem.hu. Open summer, 9am–midnight; rest of the year 11am–9pm.* This is one of the oldest and best-established restaurants on the lake, with the added bonus of an exhibition of sailing history (complete with storm simulator) upstairs. When the weather is fine, you can sit on the terrace right by the water's edge and quietly marvel at the amazing turquoise colour of the lake.

TIHANY

Beach venue

7 THE Bar – *E5* – *Kenderföld út 19. ☎ (30) 289 7802. Open mid-June–end Aug, 8am–10pm.* THE Bar is an exclusive lakeside venue belonging to the sailing club (non-members should access the bar from the lake, try a stand-up paddle board from the centre nearby). With a good view of the dancing white sails of yachts in the distance, it is the perfect place to relax and enjoy dishes (cooked sous vide) alongside local fruit and vegetables.

Tea room

😊 19 Rege Cukrászda – *E5* – *Kossuth Lajos utca 22. ☎ (30)166 4431. apatsagicukraszda.hu. Open Mon–Thu, 10am–7pm; Fri–Sun 9am–9pm.* Located in the heart of Tihany village, not far from the Benedictine Abbey Museum, this is the peninsula's most famous tea room, and not just for its splendid view of the lake. The homemade cakes are excellent and the savoury options are just as good.

Ice cream shop

20 Levendula Kézműves Fagylaltozó – *E5* – *Kossuth Lajos utca 31. ☎ (30) 166 4431. levendulafagylaltozo.hu. Open summer, 10am–6pm (Fri–Sun, 7pm).* Opposite Tihany's Benedictine Abbey as you head downhill, this ice cream parlour comes highly recommended by the locals who enjoy both its classic and more unusual flavours (lavender or camembert, anyone?).

AROUND BADACSONY

😊 The open-air venues in the vineyard estates are generally in locations offering superb views.

Wine terrace/bar

21 Csendes Dűlő Szőlőbirtok – *C6* – *Hegyalja út 43, Badacsonyörs. ☎ (70) 295 5110. Open 11am–7pm (Sat & Sun, till later).* This wine bar has a terrace with beautiful views of the vineyard, and the lake. It has also joined in with the recent trend for providing deckchairs on estate terraces, so that you can sit back and relax totally while sipping your wine with a view.

😊 22 Laposa Birtok – *C6* – *Római út 197, Badacsonytomaj. ☎ (20) 7777 133. bazaltbor.hu. Open Mon–Sun, 11am–7pm.* One of most beautiful panoramic terraces where you can also enjoy creative dishes with the wines. Sunday lunch can be ordered in summer (in advance). They aim to produce wines that could not be mistaken for those from another area.

㉓ Németh Pince – *C6* – *Római út 127, Badacsonytomaj. ☎ (70) 772 1102. nemethpince.hu.* A family-run estate that produces some award-winning wines. They are particularly proud of their late harvest wines and the sweet Badacsony ice wine.

㉔ Istvándy Pincészet – *C6* – *Hegymög dűlő, Káptalantóti. ☎ (70) 361 8421. istvandy.hu.* Another very pretty terrace perched high among the vineyards, where you can enjoy creative cuisine to accompany wines from the estate.

KESZTHELY

Tea room
㉕ Marcipán Múzeum – *A6* – *Katona József utca 19 (signposted from the palace). ☎ (83) 319 322. Open Wed-Sun, 10am-6pm. Ft180.* The marzipan museum is actually the back room of a cake shop and confectioner, where the couple who own it display their extraordinary creations, including a marzipan replica of Festetics Palace. There is a small tea room serving good cakes and homemade elderberry syrup.

VESZPRÉM

Tea room
㊲ Mackó Cukrászda – *E3* – *Megyeház tér 2. ☎ (30) 782 5232. Open 7am-7pm (Sat & Sun 9am).* Hungarians love this kind of traditional tea room, and this one in particular for the quality of its cakes and homemade desserts, which

include a delicious île flottante. Savoury snacks are also served at lunchtime.

Café
㉗ Szaléziánum Kávézó – *E3* – *Hegyalja út 69. szalezianum.hu/tea-es-kavehaz. Open 10am-6pm.* A pocket-size café and the only place to eat within the castle grounds. Cakes and small sandwiches can be enjoyed in the garden on sunny days.

SZÉKESFEHÉRVÁR

Tea room/Ice cream shop
㉘ Damniczki cukrászda – *H2* – *Fő utca 3. ☎ 340 28. damniczki.hu.* Previously located outside town and so only for those in the know, this cake shop, ice cream parlour and tea room all rolled into one made the sensible decision to open in this new venue in the centre of town. Choose from around 30 flavours of home-made ice cream and sorbet, including 'raspberry wine', winner of an award in 2013. The cakes are also delicious.

Café
㉙ Pátria Kávéház és Étterem – *H2* – *Városház tér 1. ☎ 397 089. patriakavehaz.hu. Open 9am-10pm (Fri & Sat, midnight).* Enjoying the sun from noon onwards on fine days, the lovely terrace of this historic café next to the town hall is an ideal place in which to take a break. Centrally located near all the places of interest, it might be a little plain inside, but they serve good, honest fare, and speedily.

Shopping

If Budapest is a paradise for shoppers, Lake Balaton is a dream destination for food lovers. Gourmet produce, edible delights and plenty of opportunities for gifts to take home.

Find the address on our maps using the number in the listing (1). The coordinates in red (C2) will help you to find it easily on the detachable map (inside the cover).

BUDAPEST
Detachable map

ANDRÁSSY ÚT

1 Magma – *D6* – Petőfi Sándor utca 11. M 3 Ferenciek tere. *(1) 235 0277. www.magma. hu. Open Mon–Fri, 10am–7pm, Sat 10am–3pm. Closed Sun & public holidays.* A boutique-gallery that gives Hungarian artists and designers the chance to showcase their creations: furniture, tableware (ceramic and porcelain), jewellery (pretty coloured glass rings) and bags in simple, elegant designs or inspired by Hungarian folk tradition.

2 Paprika – *D5* – Vörösmarty tér 1. M 1, 2 or 3 Deák Ferenc tér. *(20) 365 6600. *(30) 674 1331. www.paprikamarket.hu. Open 10am–8pm, Fri & Sat 10am–9pm.* Sachets of paprika, delicious wine from the Tokaj region, sweet marzipan chocolates, porcelain, jewellery, embroidery. A treasure trove for souvenir hunters.

ERZSÉBETVÁROS

3 Printa – *E5* – Rumbach Sebestyén utca 10. M 1, 2 or 3 Deák Ferenc tér. *(30) 292 0329. printa.hu. Open Mon–Sat 11am–8pm.* Located near the Rumbach Street Synagogue, this concept store is art gallery, café and designer shop all in one. With its fashionable black and white interior, it offers an array of silk screen prints and posters by emerging artists, along with eco-friendly clothes and accessories. And by buying some of these cool souvenirs you will also be supporting young local designers. It's a win-win.

FERENCVÁROS

4 Nagy Vásárcsarnok (Great Market Hall) – *E7* – Vámház krt. 1–3. M 4, 2 Fővám tér. *(1) 366 3300. www.piaconline.hu. Open Mon, 6am–5pm; Tue–Fri, 6am–6pm; Sat 6am–3pm.* The famous indoor market was opened in 1897 and has been beautifully renovated. On the ground floor are numerous stalls selling a huge choice of traditional folklore crafts and local produce: strings of paprika, garlic and onions, foie gras (prices tend to decrease the further in you go from the entrance), wines and alcohol (including the famous apricot schnapps, *barack pálinka,* or the liqueur Unicum), along with Hungarian salami. Products from the famous brand Pick are also available. The upper floor gallery is full of stalls

80

selling fast food and local crafts. Just beware of the odd tourist trap.

LAKE BALATON
Detachable map

If you fancy taking local wines home, try buying them from the wine terraces run by the estates, which all have a shop (see pp. 76–78) somewhere about the premises. If travelling by plane, regulations dictate that you will have to place bottles in the hold so make sure the packaging is secure enough.

AROUND THE LAKE (NORTH SHORE)

5 Nagyi Kamrája – **E3** – Baross Gábor utca 63. Balatonalmádi. (30) 171 2122. Open Mon, Wed–Sat, 9am–1pm, 3pm–5pm (closed Tue & Sun). The name translates as 'Grandma's Pantry' and this granny sells all kinds of delicious homemade and artisan goods: jam, sausages, farmhouse cheeses, coffee and syrups. It's a real Aladdin's Cave of edible delights.

AROUND THE LAKE (SOUTH SHORE)

7 Légli Kerámia Manufaktúra – **D7** – Epres utca 7. Balatonboglár. (70) 606 3860. www.legli.hu. Légli Pottery has been open since 1983 and makes all kinds of ceramic objects. They also specialize in oven-to-table ware, combining elegant shapes and colours with practicality. You can buy pieces in the adjacent shop.

BALATONFÜRED

8 Karolina Speiz – **E4** – Zákonyi Ferenc utca 4. (87) 583 098. karolina.hu. Open summer, 9am–11pm. Rest of the year, 9am–9pm (Fri & Sat 11.30pm). 'Karolina's Pantry' is next to its tea room (see p. 77) and sells all kinds of spices and artisan foods based on recipes from the owners' grandmother.

TIHANY

9 Tihany PIAC Placc (market near the ferry port) – **E5** – Open Sat & Sun, 8am–4pm. Part food, part flea market, this a great spot to investigate what the local producers have to offer while waiting for the ferry, or just come to browse the market itself.

10 Levendula Manufaktúra – **E5** – Batthyány utca 18. In the centre of the village, this is the place to buy Tihany lavender to take home as a gift or a fragrant reminder of your holiday.

11 Tündérsziget – **E5** – Kossuth Lajos utca 29. (30) 905 9061. Open 8am–6pm (later in summer). A clothes shop that also sells a selection of cosmetics and local gourmet food produce.

AROUND BADACSONY

6 Liliomkert Piac – **C5** – At Káptalantóti (Káli Basin). Open Sun, 9am–noon. Liliomkert market is one of the most famous farmers' markets in Hungary. People flock here, some coming from quite a distance, to enjoy the ambience and buy cheese, strudels and pálinka.

🎵

Nightlife

🕯 *Find the address on our maps using the number in the listing (❶). The coordinates in red (C2) will help you to find it easily on the detachable map (inside the cover).*

BUDAPEST
Detachable map
From opera to techno via folk music, there is a huge array of concerts and shows to enjoy in the capital in the evening, whatever your tastes, some in quite unusual locations. Check the local press for information (🕯*see p. 106*) or the leaflets distributed at the various venues. Programmes can be researched and bookings made ahead online, or tickets can be bought direct from the box offices or from the ticket vendors listed here:

Ticket Express Hungary (TEX). *In Bálna (a commercial/cultural centre).* Ⓜ *4 Fővám tér,* 🚋 *2 Zsil utca.* ✆ *(30) 505 0666. www.eventim.hu. Open Mon–Fri, 10am–6pm; Sat, 10am–3pm.*
Ticketpro. *Károly krt. 9.* Ⓜ *1, 2 or 3 Deák Ferenc tér.* ✆ *(1) 555 5515. www.ticketpro.hu. Open Mon–Fri, 9am–9pm; Sat, 10am–2pm.* Tickets are also available online.

The Andrássy út area is home to two superb music venues: the **State Opera House** and the **Franz Liszt Academy of Music** (🕯*see p. 84*). In the south of Budapest, the arts complex **MÜPA Budapest** offers an excellent programme of events. For something

a little different, head to Petőfi Bridge on the Buda side, where the ship **A38** has a permanent mooring *(see below)*. Make sure you visit one of the city's famous alternative 'ruin bars' and cafés known as **romkocsma**, which have been established in abandoned buildings in the Jewish district or in former factories and warehouses. One such is **Szimpla Kert** (🕯*see p. 84*). Another way of spending an evening with a difference is at a high octane '**sparty**', a club night at a thermal baths. Inexhaustible DJs, the latest tunes, illuminated pools, huge screens and a swimsuit dress code. Book your ticket for the Széchenyi Baths **sparty** (🕯*see p. 87*) summer season *(June–Sept)* or Lukács Baths winter season *(Oct–May; lukacsbaths.com)*.

GELLÉRTHEGY (GELLÉRT HILL)

Concerts
A38 – *Off map* – *Decommissioned cargo ship, Petőfi Bridge, Buda side.* 🚋 *4, 6 Petőfi híd.* ✆ *(1) 464 3940. www.a38.hu. Open daily, 8am–10pm.* A music venue and restaurant *(open Mon–Sat 11am–11pm)*. A concert hall and cultural centre all rolled into one, this Ukrainian cargo ship is a highlight of Budapest nightlife. There's an eclectic mix of music: pop, rock, jazz and techno. As it is anchored on the Buda side, there's a stunning view from the open-air terraces aboard the ship across to Pest and the east bank.

82

State Opera House

ANDRÁSSY ÚT

Classical music

1 Magyar Állami Operaház (Hungarian State Opera House) – **E4** – *Andrássy út 22.* Ⓜ *1 Opera.* ☎ *(1) 332 7914.* ☎ *(1) 814 7100. www. opera.hu.* A neo-Renaissance palace (1884), decorated with frescoes by the greatest Hungarian artists of the time, this is one of the most prestigious opera houses in Europe. The biggest names in music play here. Performances take place in the Erkel Theatre and other venues.

2 Liszt Ferenc Zeneművészeti Egyetem (Franz Liszt Academy of Music) – **E4** – *Liszt Ferenc tér 8.* Ⓜ *1 Oktogon.* ☎ *(1) 462 4600. zeneakademia.hu.* Founded by the eponymous Hungarian composer in 1907, the academy remains the capital's premier concert venue. It occupies a beautiful Art Nouveau building with stained-glass windows, mosaics and sparkling crystal chandeliers. Audiences will be rewarded with performances by the best symphony orchestras in the country at very affordable prices. And if you're nearby at rehearsal time, you might hear strains of lovely music echoing around the neighbourhood.

Aperitif with a view

3 360 Bar – **E4** – *Andrássy út 39.* Ⓜ *1 Opera.* ☎ *(30) 356 3047. 360bar. hu.* Open 2pm–midnight (Thu–Sat, 2pm–2am.) Budapest's most beautiful rooftop bar, on the old Párizsi (Paris) Nagyáruház department store building, is the perfect spot to watch the sun go down, drink in hand. In the colder months, do the same from the warmth of one of the transparent domes in the Igloo Garden.

ERZSÉBETVÁROS

Wine tasting

4 Doblo Wine & Bar – **E5** – *Dob utca 20.* Ⓜ *2 Astoria.* ☎ *(20) 398 8863. www.budapestwine.com. Open 2pm–2am; Thu–Sat, 2pm–4am.* A great place in which to discover Hungary's wines. Try the sweet wine from the Tokaj region or fruity red wines from Szekszárd. Whatever you choose, you should also enjoy the bar's bohemian ambience with its backdrop of warmly lit, bare-brick walls, lined with bottles of wine, paintings and photos.

Romkocsma (Ruin bar)

5 Szimpla Kert – **E5** – *Kazinczy utca 14.* Ⓜ *2 Astoria.* ☎ *(20) 261 8669. szimpla.hu. Open noon–4am; Sun, 9am–4am.* Upcycled furniture, exposed pipes and ducting, lit by small coloured lamps, a pretty courtyard … all the features of a real *romkocsma*. Szimpla Kert is an institution, but go for a drink and the music rather than to eat. DJs and live shows (from 8pm) in the evening.

LIPÓTVÁROS

Jazz club

6 Budapest Jazz Club – **D2** – *Hollán Ernő utca. 7.* Ⓜ *3 Nyugati pályaudvar.* 🚊 *4, 6 Jászai Mari tér.* ☎ *(1) 798 7289. www.bjc.hu/home.*

84

Open Mon–Thu, 10am–midnight (Fri & Sat 2am); Sun 4pm–midnight. The most famous jazz club in Budapest, with live shows (international artists) and jam sessions every day. The music starts at 8pm but arrive earlier and eat in the café or bistro. Enjoy the music with a glass of excellent wine in hand if you so choose.

LAKE BALATON
Detachable map

AROUND THE LAKE (NORTH SHORE)

Wine bar
8 **Terazza Bistro & Bar** – *B4* – *Csalogány utca 7. Sümeg. ℘ (30) 813 8447. terazza.hu. Open Thu, noon–10pm; Fri–Sun, 11.30am–11pm.* Enjoy a drink among the greenery on the terrace, with a stunning view across to the medieval Sümeg castle.

AROUND THE LAKE (SOUTH SHORE)

Open-air cinema
7 **Club Aliga Kertmozi** – *F4* – *Aligai út 1. Balatonvilágos. ℘ (88) 573 230.* Balaton's largest open-air cinema with more than 600 seats (there's a roof but the sides are open). A local institution.

Ruin bar
9 **Lógó Üveg** – *F5* – *Fő utca 55. Siófok. ℘ (70) 945 7677. logouveg. hu. Open 5pm–midnight (Fri & Sat, 2am).* Siófok's first ruin bar with a cool, bunker-like interior, with dozens of empty bottles dangling from the ceiling. Lógó Üveg means 'hanging glass'. Alternative-style concerts some weekends.

Club
10 **Pub–Lik** – *E5* – *Széchenyi utca 10. Balatonföldvár. ℘ (84) 340 328. Open 11am–4am.* DJ nights, live concerts or broadcasts of live sporting events, this is one of Lake Balaton's top nightspots. It often sells out.

BALATONFÜRED

Wine bars
11 **Kredenc** – *E4* – *Blaha Lujza utca 7. ℘ (20) 518 9960. kredencborbisztro. hu.* Opened by a former member of a techno band, this bar is a magnet for young locals. The choice of music (bossa nova, jazz and swing) is as impressive as the wine list, sourced mostly from the Balaton area.
12 **Matróz** – *E4* – *Écsy László utca 5. ℘ (70) 708 9206. Open Jun–Aug, Fri & Sat, 8pm–4am (closed Sun–Thu).* Hip locals enjoy this wine bar in a beautiful former villa, where the terrace turns into a dance floor until the early hours.

AROUND BADACSONY

Wine bar
13 **FrissTerasz** – *C6* – *Római út 179. Badacsonytomaj. ℘ (20) 313 5173. frissterasz.hu. Open summer, noon–midnight.* The Laposa family (**⚓***see p. 78*) opened another panoramic venue here, which is a bit more fun and relaxed. Concerts in high season.

85

Visiting the baths

Hungary's thermal baths are one of its great attractions, particularly in Budapest and the Lake Balaton region, where there are numerous baths and spa complexes to choose from. They are something of an institution for some people. Some baths focus on treatments and some on relaxation, while others have transformed into large, family-friendly water parks.

Prices

Entrance to the baths is cheaper on **weekdays** than at the weekend and some spas offer a reduced rate for the end of the day. The prices given here are for the minimum daily rate, but half-day tickets are available at some baths. Weekends are the busiest times.

⊛ You can obtain a 20% reduction on the entrance fee to a number of baths with the **Budapest Card** (⌚*see p. 96*).

⊛ Some baths do not take credit cards, so take cash with you, especially if you plan to have a treatment (allow around Ft6,000 for a 20min massage). You can normally choose between the cabin rate (changing rooms where you can leave your belongings safely) or the cheaper locker rate. You will be given a wristband or an electronic card to lock and unlock your locker. The prices given in our descriptions of the baths are for adults. If you have children with you, enquire beforehand as some baths refuse entry to those under 14 years of age.

Equipment

You will need swimwear, towel, flip-flops or plastic sandals, a swimming cap (if you want to use the swimming pools) and a waterproof bag (for toiletries). You can generally hire or purchase some key items.

⌚ *Find the address on our maps using the number in the listing (❶). The coordinates in red (C2) will help you to find it easily on the detachable map (inside the cover).*

BUDAPEST

Detachable map

⊛ The Budapest baths (10 spas and 7 thermal bath houses) are managed by Budapest Spas; see **www.spasbudapest.com** *(in English)* for details on 11 bathing venues, including location and information on different pools and temperatures. For information on 'sparties' (⌚*see p. 82*), see **www.bathsbudapest.com**. These are the pool parties (swimsuit discos) organized at weekends.

GELLÉRTHEGY (GELLÉRT HILL)

☺ ❶ **Gellért Gyógyfürdő** – *D8* – *Kelenhegyi út 4. Entrance in the road to the right of Hotel Gellért.* Ⓜ *4,* Ⓣ *19, 41, 47, 48, 49, 56, 56A Szent Gellért tér.* ☏ *(1) 466 6166. www.gellertbath. hu. Open 6am–8pm. Mixed baths from Ft6,300.* They might be in need of a little refurbishment, but Gellért Baths are some of the most spectacular in the capital. Massages are available and there's a VIP section. The waters (slightly radioactive) are said to be good for easing rheumatism and osteoarthritis.

VÁROSLIGET (CITY PARK)

😊 ② **Széchenyi Gyógyfürdő** – *G1* – *Állatkerti körút 11.* Ⓜ *1 Széchenyi fürdő.* ☎ *(1) 363 3210. www. szechenyibath.hu. Mixed baths, open 6am–10pm. From Ft5,900.* In the heart of Városliget (City Park). Outside you'll find a thermal whirlpool, an Olympic size swimming pool, a thermal pool (38°C/100°F), solarium and restaurant. Inside there are several baths, from cold to very warm. Treatments and massages are provided in booths (♿*see p. 24*).

LAKE BALATON
Detachable map

A number of the baths here have developed their family-friendly activities in addition to their spas.

AROUND THE LAKE (SOUTH SHORE)

♿ ③ **Zalakarosi Fürdő** – *A8* – *Termál út 4. Zalakaros.* ☎*(93) 340 420. hellozalakaros.hu/en. Ft3,000/4,800 per day, depending on whether you want to use all or part of the water park.* The most popular and family-friendly in the Balaton region. Apart from the thermal bathing pools and the therapy and wellness centres, there's a wave pool and great facilities for children (water slides, and so on).

④ **Csiszta Fürdő** – *C7* – *Fürdő tér. Buzsák.* ☎ *(30) 503 9612. csisztafurdo.hu. Ft1,800 per day.* Opened in the 1960s, these modern and well-maintained baths have 5 pools, including a children's pool, as well as a children's playground, a sauna, restaurant and café.

♿ ⑤ **Galerius Élményfürdő** – *F5* – *Szent László utca 183. Siófok–Szabadifürdő.* ☎ *(84) 506 580. galerius-furdo.hu. Ft2,900/3,600 per day.* A haven for sauna fans (includes a bio-sauna), there are a dozen pools (some geo-thermal), giant slides and a jacuzzi big enough for 21 people.

HÉVÍZ

⑥ **Hévízgyógyfürdő (Hévíz thermal lake and spa)** – *A6* – Swim or float in the world's largest thermal lake. ♿*See p. 48.*

♿ ⑦ **Kehida Termál Gyógy–és Élményfürdő (Kehida Termál Adventure Bath and Spa)** – *A6* – *Kossuth utca 62, at Kehidakustány (15km/9mi north-west of Hévíz).* ☎ *(83) 534 500. kehidatermal.hu/en. Ft5,300/2,900 per day, depending on which zone you choose.* A fantastic family-friendly thermal water area with slides, lazy river and thermal pools, wellness and therapy centres.

SZÉKESFEHÉRVÁR

⑧ **Árpád Fürdő** – *H2* – *Kossuth u. 12.* ☎ *(22) 814 400. fehervar-arpadfurdo. hu. Open 9am–10pm. Ft3,500/4,500 per day.* Renovated in 2010, these Art Nouveau baths (1905) have retained some of their lovely period features, Perfect for an afternoon of relaxation.

Where to stay

☻ It will be no surprise to learn that booking ahead is recommended in and around Lake Balaton during the high season, between April and end October. Outside these months you will need to check if venues are open. However, the choice of out-of-season accommodation is gradually increasing.

☝Find the address on our maps using the number in the listing (①). The coordinates in red (C2) will help you to find it easily on the detachable map (inside the cover).

BUDAPEST
Detachable map

VÁRNEGYED (CASTLE DISTRICT)

Ft30,000-60,000
☻ ① **Baltazár** – *B4* – *Országház utca 31.* 🚌 *16, 16A, 116 Bécsi kapu tér,* Ⓜ *2 Széll Kálmán tér.* ℘ *(1) 300 7051. baltazarbudapest.com.* 🛏 🅿 *Ft6,500 per day. 11 rooms, Ft29,000/55,000* ☕. ✗. A charming boutique hotel with very comfortable rooms in a quiet location. It also has an excellent restaurant with a terrace and pleasant wine bar.

BELVÁROS

Ft30,000-60,000
② **Gerlóczy Kávéház. Rooms de Lux** – *E5* – *Gerlóczy utca 1.* Ⓜ *3 Ferenciek tere,* Ⓜ *2 Astoria.* ℘ *(1) 501 4000.*

www.gerloczy.hu. 🛏. *19 rooms. Ft28,800/Ft52,440.* ☕ *Ft3,885.* ✗. A stone's throw from the Danube, this is a small hotel above a café with a turn-of-the-century feel, fusing retro charm with an eye for detail and high standards.

ERZSÉBETVÁROS

Ft35,000-45,000
③ **Roombach** – *E5* – *Rumbach Sebestyén utca 14.* Ⓜ *1, 2 or 3 Deák Ferenc tér.* ℘ *(1) 413 0253. roombach. com.* 🛏 🅿 *Ft4,850 per day.* ♿. *98 rooms, Ft35,200/41,700* ☕. Ideally located in the heart of the capital's most hyped district, you can walk from here to the city's major sites. The rooms are small but comfortable and spotless. A friendly welcome and a buffet-style breakfast.

LAKE BALATON
Detachable map

AROUND THE LAKE (NORTH SHORE)

Ft20,000–30,000
④ **Villa Millenium** – *E3* – *Mikszáth utca 5. Balatonalmádi.* ℘ *(30) 461 0229. villamillennium.hu. Ft23,900* ☕. A very good guesthouse that has been completely renovated. It occupies the handsome villa that housed the first guesthouse in the vicinity. The lovely garden is a bonus.

AROUND THE LAKE (SOUTH SHORE)

Ft25,000–40,000

5 Kristinus Borbirtok – **B8** – Hunyadi utca 99, Kéthely. (85) 539 014. kristinus.hu. 10 rooms. Ft26,200/36,700 ☐. ✕ Ft3,690/6,990 (Gastro Bistrot open Wed–Sun). Stay in one of the upmarket designer rooms on the Kirstinus wine estate and dine in the excellent Gastro Bistrot (a fine-dining restaurant is also in the pipeline). The minimalist design of the winery allows the stunning landscape to take centre stage. A great place to stay.

Ft30,000–40,000

6 Jókai Villa Hotel – **F5** – Batthyány utca 2, Siófok. (84) 506 798. jokaivilla.com. 12 rooms. Ft32,400/38,600 ☐. Named after the author Mór Jókai (see p. 36), who spent his last summer here, this beautiful and majestic villa near the centre of Siófok and the beaches has retained its old world charm. The garden is lovely.

BALATONFÜRED

Ft20,000–30,000

7 Gombás Kúria – **E4** – Arácsi út 94 (30min walk from the lake). (30) 9317 522. gombaskuria.hu. 11 rooms. Ft22,700/26,000 ☐. This former 18C wine estate in a quiet location has retained its character. The simple but comfortable rooms enclose a pleasant garden; there's a small playground for children.

TIHANY

Ft20,000–30,000

8 Kora Panzió – **E5** – Halász utca 5. (20) 9443 982. tihanykora.hu. 6 rooms. Ft22,700/26,000 ☐. In a quiet wooded area near the lake, 2km/1.25 mi from the village, this small guesthouse earns plaudits for its cleanliness and pretty garden with a small swimming pool. There's also a barbecue area.

AROUND BADACSONY

Ft20,000–30,000

9 Óbester Panzió – **C6** – Római út 203. Badacsonytomaj. (30) 213 0225. obester.hu. 8 rooms (and 2 apartments), Ft19,900/23,900 ☐. Run by a Hungarian-Swedish family, along with their cats and dogs, this former farm is one of our favourite locations. Simple and comfortable, the rooms look out onto the peaceful vineyards and lakes. Barbecues in the evenings and books about the area to leaf through beside the lovely garden.

Ft30,000–40,000

10 Kreinbacher Birtok – **B2** – Somló hegy. 8481 Somlóvásárhely (near Somló Hill). (88) 236 420. kreinbacher.hu. 16 rooms, from Ft32,000 ☐. ✕ Dinner tasting menu Ft7,990/10,990, à la carte Ft2,990/5,990. A wine estate with a hotel, in an ultra modern style that manages to blend well with its surroundings. A fine wine bar and restaurant, too, with a terrace.

Planning your trip

Train on the shore of Lake Balaton
© gehringj/iStock

Know before you go

ENTRY REQUIREMENTS

Documents – Visitors are advised to keep their passport with them at all times as proof of ID and will need to show it when checking in at accommodation.

Visa – UK, US, Irish, Australian, New Zealand and Canadian citizens can stay for up to 90 days without a visa provided they are in possession of a valid passport. For more specific details, see your embassy's website *(p. 100)*.

Customs – Under the terms of the Schengen Agreement, there are no customs' controls when crossing the border from one country in the European Union to another. If arriving from a non-EU country, you must pass through customs and declare items you are carrying in excess of the limits (200 cigarettes, 1 litre spirits or 4 litres still wine, more than €10,000 in cash or the equivalent in another currency). For more detailed information on import and export regulations see: www.iatatravelcentre.com, or en.nav.gov.hu

Driving licence – Some foreign driving licences are accepted, but require a certified Hungarian translation. To avoid having to translate your licence, carry both your licence and an International Driving Permit. (UK visitors: a pink photocard UK licence is accepted but otherwise an International Driving Permit is required). If driving your own car, you must also carry your passport, a document showing proof of ownership (such as the V5C certificate for UK drivers), proof of insurance/ Green Card (*see Car rental, p. 93; Driving/Parking p. 100*).

TO BUDAPEST BY PLANE

Budapest's international airport is **Budapest Liszt Ferenc** (*see p. 3*).

Regular airlines

Major international airlines (subject to change) flying to Budapest include:

American Airlines: www.aa.com
Air Canada: www.aircanada.com
Air France: www.airfrance.com
British Airways: www.britishairways.com
Brussels Airlines: www.brusselsairlines.com
KLM: www.klm.com
Lufthansa: www.lufthansa.com
Norwegian Air: www.norwegian.com

Low-cost airlines

Budget airlines (subject to change), include:

EasyJet: www.easyjet.com
Jet2: www.jet2.com
LOT: www.lot.com
Ryanair: www.ryanair.com
Wizz Air: www.wizzair.com

You can research and compare times/ prices at: www.google.com/flights

LEFT LUGGAGE

The website **luggagepals.com** allows you to find and pay online for bag storage offered by shops and cafés in Budapest. Prices quoted in euros: €5 (around £4.20/US$5.50) per day small bag/case and €6 (around £5/US$6.50) to store a large bag. However, the service is not yet up and running in the Balaton area.

MONEY

Currency – The unit of currency in Hungary is the **forint**, abbreviated to **Ft** within the country and **HUF** abroad.

Euro – Although Hungary is part of the EU, it has not yet decided to adopt the euro. Given the fluctuation in exchange rates for the forint, some tourist attractions quote prices in euros.

Some hotels, restaurants and other outlets accept euros as well as forints. However, if you pay in euros you may be given forints as change and find that you are in effect paying more than if you settle a bill in forints. We recommend researching the situation at the time of travel, when you can decide if it is worth taking any euros with you.

Changing money – Money can be changed in banks, bureau de change, travel agents and in hotels.

You can also find ATMs at the airport near baggage reclaim (although the rates are generally not very good). Never under any circumstances change money in the street, even if someone approaches you offering good rates: there's a strong risk of being scammed and such transactions are also illegal. (*See Banks p. 95.*)

Credit cards – Payment by credit card is very common. Credit cards such as Diners Club, Cirrus, Visa, American Express, Euro/MasterCard, JCB, Visa are accepted in most places.

ATMs – Indicated by the word *Bankomat,* ATMs are numerous in Budapest, but less so in the towns and villages of the Balaton area. Bearing this in mind, you may wish to obtain some forints in cash in advance before you travel to Lake Balaton. There is often an option to choose English instructions on the ATM screen.

BUDGETING

Staying in Budapest is generally a little more expensive than in the rest of Hungary (say around 20% more expensive). A beer or glass of the house lemonade (50cl/17 US fl oz) costs around Ft7/800, a small glass of good wine Ft4/500, a pastry around Ft4/500 in an average bar, café or tea room, or double that in a more upmarket place. Coffee is usually excellent and costs around Ft400. If you keep an eye out for good deals, it is possible, or even quite easy, to have a meal for Ft3,000–4,000 and to find a room for under Ft17,000 for two at a *panzió*, b&b or guesthouse, many of which give the hotels a good run for their money. If you want to treat yourself, a luxury room will cost in the region of Ft30,000–40,0000, while a more expensive meal will be around Ft10,000–16,000.

CAR RENTAL

All the major international companies have offices in Budapest and offer the normal rental service with good quality cars. Most of the low-cost rental firms propose additional insurance, which doubles the rental cost and makes their rates far less attractive. If you don't take it, you agree, in the event of a claim, to pay a high fee (around €1,000). It will be applied irrespective of any damage, even just for a tiny scratch. You have been warned! You must have a valid driving licence. (*See also p. 100*).

SEASONS AND CLIMATE

Hungary has a Continental climate: summers are often very hot, with temperatures in excess of 30°C/86°F between July and August; winters can be harsh with daytime temperatures often remaining below freezing, especially during January. You may find spring and autumn the most comfortable times (and the lake won't be as busy then as in high season). Some hotels in the Balaton area close between November and April. When a big event is being held (such as the Formula 1 Grand Prix), the hotels soon fill up, in both the capital and around Lake Balaton.

FIND OUT MORE

Before you leave

The following sites are in English:
budapestinfo.hu: official tourist website.

spiceofeurope.com: official website of the Hungarian Tourism Agency.
wowhungary.com: official website of the Hungarian Tourism Agency.

welovebudapest.com: bars, restaurants, shopping, nightlife... Plenty of useful, reliable information.
spottedbylocals.com: recommendations from the locals.
budapestcitycard.com: buy a Budapest Card *(p. 96)* before arriving.
funzine.hu: information on Lake Balaton *(p. 106)*.

In Hungary

Contact any of the **Tourinform** offices, which are part of the Hungarian Tourist Office (tourinform.hu), for information during your stay on places to visit, accommodation, etc.

In Budapest

The Tourist Office issues the free **Budapest Guide** in English and a city map for tourists.
Tourinform – They have several offices in the city.

Around Lake Balaton

The free **Funzine** produces a Balaton special, available in tourist offices. All the towns around the lake have a **Tourinform** office *(see info. for each town in the Discover section)*; smaller localities usually have them, too (often shut in winter). (*See Tourist publications p. 106.*)

Basic information

BANKS

Commission – Bureaus de change in the town centres and railway stations often offer the best rates. The banks generally charge average rates of commission, while changing money at hotels and airports is usually less advantageous. ATMs are a useful way of obtaining cash in forints; Hungarian bank ATMs often don't charge a local fee (unlike non-bank ATMs), but commission and perhaps currency conversion will normally be charged by your home bank, so check on the rates before leaving.

Hungarian currency – Forints are available in notes of Ft500, 1,000, 2,000, 5,000, 10,000 and 20,000; and in coins of Ft5, 10, 20, 50, 100 and 200. Keep an eye on the number of zeros to avoid being caught out – you can come across a few dishonest people all over the world.

See Business hours p. 97.

BEACHES

While there is plenty to keep you occupied around the lake, the beaches are its biggest attraction. They are numerous, but here are a few of our favourites, with lifeguards on duty, good amenities and suitable for children, some with shallow water perfect for little ones.

Around the lake

Lidó Strand, at Vonyarcvashegy – *8km/5mi east of Keszthely, north shore*. A range of facilities for watersports. Grass.

Diási Játékstrand – *5km/3.5mi east of Keszthely, north shore*. Lots of equipment, open-air games (giant chess, mini golf….). Grass.

Fonyód Beach – *10km/6mi east of Balatonboglár, south shore*. With a lovely view of the volcanic mountains of the north shore, this beach is one of the few to have a stretch of sand.

Main beach, at Siófok – *Next to the marina, south shore*. Packed in summer. There's also an area with sand and palm trees.

See also the Discovering section of the guide p. 28, 29, 37, 42 and 52.

Balatonfüred

Of the three beaches in Balatonfüred, we recommend **Kisfaludy Strand**.

EMERGENCY NUMBERS

Ambulance, Police, Fire (Europe-wide number): ☏ **112**

Ambulance (Hungary internal number): ☏ **104**

Police (Hungary): ☏ **107**

Fire brigade (Hungary): ☏ **105**

Doctor 24hr (Főnix SOS): ☏ (1) 203-3615

Pharmacist 24hr: Teréz Patika - Teréz krt. 41 (**E3**) - ☏ (1) 311 4439

SOS dentist: ☏ (1) 317 6600

It is a paying beach (with some sand) in the holiday season, but it is clean with good facilities. *(balatonfuredistrandok.hu; summer open 8.30am–7pm.)*

Tihany
Sajkodi Strand – *As you approach Tihany Peninsula from the southwest.* Surrounded by trees, steps lead down to the water. Grass. Can be busy.

Keszthely
Helikon and Városi beaches charge for entry in high season *(8.30am–7pm, Ft800/400)*, but the facilities are good and suitable for children.

BOAT TRIPS

In Budapest
A number of agencies specialize in trips on the water, including:
Legenda – *Quay/pier n° 7, Vigadó tér.* **M** *1 Vörösmarty tér,* **Tram** *2 Vigadó tér.* ℘ *317 2203. legenda.hu.*
A trip (daytime) of 1hr 10min, from Ft4,500.
Mahart PassNave – *Belgrád rakpart.* **M** *4 Fővám tér,* **Tram** *2 Fővám tér.* ℘ *484 4013. mahartpassnave.hu.*
Have dinner on board. From Ft12,000 (reduction with the Budapest Card).

Lake Balaton
Known for its yachting fraternity and regattas, the lake is also used for boat cruises.

Balatoni Hajózási Zrt. – *Krúdy sétány 2 (Siófok).* ℘ *(84) 310 050. balatonihajozas.hu.* This company serves 17 towns on Lake Balaton, between spring and autumn. Try a

mini cruise (sunset or stargazing), or one with with an on-board event.

BUDAPEST CARD

The **Budapest Kártya/Budapest Card**, a discount card for tourists, can make good sense; it provides unlimited travel on public transport within the city, free access to a number of museums and baths, and discounts at some restaurants and places of interest.

Its benefits in more detail include:
– Free travel by public transport. (Metro, bus, trolleybus, trams, HÉV suburban trains); but not the Buda funicular (⛰*see Sikló, p. 16*).
(For travel beyond the city, buy an extension ticket at your departure point while presenting your Budapest Card.)
– Free or reduced admission to many museums and cultural sites.
– Reductions on ticket prices to some shows, and in some shops, cafés, pubs and spas.
– Reduction on some car hire and bike hire on Margaret Island (Margitsziget).
For more information see: www.budapestinfo.hu/card-info

in Tourinform offices *(p. 94)*, ☻ You can buy the card at the airport, in Tourinform offices *(p. 94)*, in the larger metro stations and at travel agents, but also online from: **budapest-card.com**, a 5% reduction.
Budapest Card prices: Ft6,490/24hrs, Ft9,990/48hrs and Ft12,990/72hrs. Don't forget to date and sign your card before you use it. You will also receive a small guide with information on where/how to use it.

BUSINESS HOURS

Shops – Usually open Mon–Fri, 10am–6pm (Sat, 2pm). Some shops remain open on Saturday afternoon and Sunday, notably in the malls or tourist areas, such as the Buda Castle district and Váci utca (street) in Budapest, and in some of the larger towns around Lake Balaton. Food stores are often open 7am–9pm (Sat, 2pm). The small 24hr stores can be identified by the sign 'Non Stop'.
Almost all shops are shut 25 and 26 December.
Banks – Open Mon–Thu, 8am–5pm; Fri 8am–2pm.
Museums and places of interest – Usually open 10am–6pm (some are shut Mondays and public holidays).

Post offices – Open Mon–Fri, 8am–6pm, Sat 8am–noon. In Budapest, the post office at Teréz krt. 51 (near Nyugati Pályaudvar railway station, **E3**) has longer hours: 7am–8pm, Sun, 8am–6pm. In Lake Balaton there's at least one post office in each locality, villages included.

CHILDREN

Safe and clean, Hungary is a terrific destination for families, and Hungarians are very welcoming to children generally speaking. Activities that children will find fun are marked in this guide with the symbol 👫.
In **Budapest**, activities to do with kids include visiting a thermal baths

97

© Hungarian Tourism Agency

Vineyards near Lake Balaton

complex (unless otherwise indicated, children are allowed in the swimming pools), and there are a number of places where children can run around in the open air (such as Margaret Island), or stop for a tasty slice of cake or an ice cream at one of the many pavement cafés.

As for **Lake Balaton**, it is ideal for families. Many of its beaches have good facilities for children and are perfect for young swimmers – the water is very shallow in parts, with the lakebed shelving so gradually in some areas that you can wade out quite happily for several hundred metres. The water parks are another attraction popular with children (giant water slides, wave machines…) and are often coupled with thermal baths for the grown-ups (see p. 86).

CYCLING

Budapest
Cars are not allowed on Margaret Island, which makes it the perfect place for two-wheeled transport. Bikes are available to rent near the southern entrance to the island, and guided tours by bike are also available; it's a lovely way to explore and learn about the island at the same time.

⊙ MOL Bubi (molbubi.bkk.hu) operates a **public bike rental scheme**. Pick up (and return) one of their green bikes from any docking station (most are on the Pest side of the city). Ft500/24hrs, Ft1,000/72hrs, Ft2,000/1 week.)

Around Lake Balaton
Balatoni Bringakörút (Lake Balaton Cycle Trail) – Since its launch in 2002, this has become one of the most celebrated cycle paths in the country. Around 200km/124mi long and well signposted, most of the trail (north shore) ensures the cyclist is riding on dedicated paths separated from traffic. Along the south shore, the trail also uses normal side roads and passes through some seaside resorts. Elsewhere, it crosses some wooded terrain, while some gravel paths are also to be expected, but a specialist bike is not required.

Other cycle paths – There are more than 50 cycle paths around the lake region (six are mountain bike trails and nine are long-distance routes). There are paths for all levels of experience. The tourist offices in each locality can supply information on hiring bikes and provide free cycle path maps with descriptions of the routes.

⊙ Some stages of the cycle trails are quite long. i.e. the distance you must cycle between places where you can find refreshment. Bear this in mind in summer, when temperatures are often high and can easily reach 40°C/104°F. Be sure to take enough food and water with you. That said, where a path hugs the shoreline, there is often a chance to cool off with a dip in the lake, so don't forget your swimming costume, too!

HUNGARY, THE WELLSPRING OF WONDERS

HÉVÍZ

DRIVING/PARKING

Budapest
As in all the capital cities of the world, traffic is congested at peak times. If you arrive in Budapest by car, it's a good idea to park as soon as you can and take advantage of the excellent public transport network. You normally have to pay to park on the street during the week (at a parking meter, or online via a smartphone app), but you should find it's free at weekends.

Around Lake Balaton
To drive to Lake Balaton from Budapest, you have the option of taking the motorway/highway in which case you need to buy an electronic sticker/vignette (Ft3,500/10 days, Ft4,780/1 month, Ft42,980/1 year). You can buy one at highway petrol stations, or in advance online (you'll need to know your registration number).
Information at: hungary-vignette.eu.
General information: rac.co.uk/drive/travel/country/hungary/
☺ When hiring a car, ask if the price includes the motorway vignette. It often does. (&*See Car rental p. 93.*)

EATING OUT

As in Budapest, you can find somewhere to eat around the lake at almost any time of day and choose between different types of restaurant:
– **étterem**: a classic restaurant with fixed and à la carte menus;
– **büfé**: fast-food, serve yourself, choosing from sandwiches, cakes, hot and cold drinks;
– **vendéglő**: a more informal brasserie-style restaurant.
Once you are seated in a restaurant, someone will normally give you a menu and ask what you would like to drink.
& *See Tipping p. 106.*
A **traditional meal** generally includes soup, a robust main course, a dessert, a drink and a coffee to finish (choosing between capuccino and espresso).
&*See Goulash and paprika p. 118, Where to eat p. 66 and the detachable map inside the cover to locate the restaurants we have selected.*
Michelin Guide: Main Cities of Europe *also provides a selection of restaurants in Budapest, including several with Michelin stars.*

ELECTRICITY

As elsewhere in Europe, the standard voltage is 220V.

EMBASSIES

British Embassy
Füge utca 5–8, Budapest
℘ (1) 266 2888
www.gov.uk/world/organisations/british-embassy-budapest
Embassy of Ireland
Szabadság ter 7, Budapest
℘(1) 301 4960
www.dfa.ie/irish-embassy/hungary/
US Embassy
Szabadság tér 12, Budapest
℘ (1) 475 4400
https://hu.usembassy.gov/embassy/

Embassy of Canada
Ganz utca 12–14, Budapest
☎ (1) 392 3360
www.canadainternational.gc.ca/
hungary-hongrie
Australian Embassy
Now closed. Enquiries can be
directed to the embassy in Vienna
https://austria.embassy.gov.au
☎ + (43) 1 506 740, or call the
Consular Emergency Call Centre in
Canberra direct ☎ + (61) 2 6261 3305
New Zealand Embassy
Enquiries can be directed to the
embassy in Vienna.
☎ + (43) 1 505 3020
www.mfat.govt.nz/austria.

GOLF

Some fine courses are to be found in
the undulating landscape around Lake
Balaton:
Royal Balaton Golf Club – *Vászolyi
út 33, at Balatonudvari (north shore).*
☎ *(87) 549 200. balatongolf.hu.
On-site restaurant.* The first course to
open in the region (2008); 18 holes
with a beautiful view of the lake.
Golfclub Imperial Balaton –
At Balatongyörök (north shore).
☎ *(83) 346 031. golfclubimperial.hu.
Restaurant.* Situated between Hévíz
and Badacsony, this course opened
fairly recently; 9 holes, and with a
private beach!

GUIDED TOURS

Budapest
A number of agencies specialize in
walking tours. Ask about these at the
Tourinform offices.

Walking tours
Absolute Walking Tours – ☎ (1) 269
3843. www.absolutetours.com.
Several themed tours, from around
€35 (£30/US$38) for 3hrs. Plus bike
and Segway tours.

Bike & Segway tours
Yellow Zebra Bikes – Sütő utca 2.
Ⓜ 1, 2 or 3 Deák Ferenc tér. ☎ (1) 269
3843. yellowzebrabikes.com. From
€29 (£24/US$31) for 4hrs with a café
stop. They also offer walking tours.
BudaBike Tours – ☎ (1) 70 671 1274.
www.budabike.com. Book 1 day
minimum in advance. Five tours of
2/3 hrs (from around €22/£18/US$24)
including one tour in the evening to
see the city lit up at night.

In a Trabant
Cityrama – Báthory utca 22. ☎ 302
4382. www.cityrama.hu. A self-
drive tour in a Trabant (remember
your driving licence) costs around
€70/£59/US$75 for two.

In a tuk tuk
Budapest Tuk tuk – ☎ (70) 257 3020.
budapesttuktuk.com/en/. A fun way
of touring the city; 2/3 people from
around €37/£30/US$40 per person.

Amphibious bus
RiverRide– Széchenyi tér. ☎ 332
2555. www.riverride.com. A trip in an
amphibious bus across the streets …
and the Danube! From Ft9,000.

Around Lake Balaton
♿*See Boat Trips, p. 96.*

HEALTH

Take a good mosquito repellent with
you to Lake Balaton as the local

mozzies are numerous and greedy! And be aware also of the possibility of ticks lurking in tall grass. Apart from that, there are no other particular hazards. Visitors to Hungary are entitled to free emergency care in the event of an accident, but otherwise medical care needs to be paid for, so before your trip make sure you have adequate insurance cover. *(Emergency numbers, see p. 95.)*

HIKING AND WALKING

Along with cycling and water sports, hiking is very popular around Lake Balaton, making use of around 60 marked trails suitable for all levels. These include three routes on the Tihany Peninsula (see p. 42), but you can find walking trails at nearly all the Lake Balaton localities.
Most of the tourist offices can supply free leaflets (often just simple photocopies) marked with detailed routes. From wetlands to forests, and from volcanic mountains (Badacsony, p. 44) and lake islands (Kányavári, p. 33) to interesting geological landscapes (Hegyestű, p. 46), Lake Balaton is a very rewarding region for walkers.

ICE SKATING

Some people skate on the frozen Lake Balaton in winter, but we wouldn't recommend it for safety reasons. There are a few dedicated ice rinks dotted around the lake, however.
Szigliget – *(north shore) Soponyai út, near the municipal beach.* A large rink (30m/98ft x 17m/55ft). And there's

even a sauna for warming up chilly toes afterwards.
BL Yachtclub, at Balatonlelle – *(south shore) Köztársaság utca 36–38. blyc.hu.* This rink also has a sauna for rounding off your exercise alfresco with a little warming relaxation.

INTERNET

Good news for those who can't live without it, Budapest is a highly connected capital. Bars, cafés, restaurants and hotels mostly offer free access (just ask for the code if it is not displayed). Even river buses offer free wifi. You'll find the same level of ultra connection around Lake Balaton, where the smallest café posts its password for all to see (often on a slate behind the counter).

MARKETS

In Budapest
Don't miss the celebrated covered market in the **Great Market Hall** (1897) which has been beautifully restored (see Shopping p. 80).

Around Lake Balaton
Most towns and villages have their own market. Known for the quality of the produce on offer, the farmers' markets are in full swing in season, especially the two that are best known: **Liliomkert** at Káptalantóti *(a few miles north of Badacsonytomaj, on the north shore)* on Sundays (a farmers' market with bric-à-brac and crafts), and the market that is held near the ferry terminal in **Tihany** on Saturdays and Sundays, selling

local food produce and bric-à-brac
(&see p. 81). There is also a market at
Balatonföldvár (daily, 7.30am–1pm,
next to the railway station), between
beginning April and mid-October,
with a pretty view of the lake. And
once the air starts to get a little
fresher, you'll find mulled wine
making an appearance on some stalls.

PHONE CALLS

From abroad to Hungary
& 00 + 36 (the country code) + area
code (such as 1 for Budapest).

From Hungary to abroad
To the UK & 00 44; US and Canada
00 + 1; Ireland 00 + 353; Australia
00 + 61; New Zealand 00 + 64; South
Africa 00 + 27 ... followed by the area
code (omitting the first number), then
the number of person you are calling.

From Budapest to the provinces
& 06 + area code + number.

From the provinces to Budapest
& 06 +1 + the 7-digit number.

Within Budapest
Just dial the number you wish to
call, which should consist of 7 digits
(without any prefix).

Mobile/Cell phones
All visitors should check roaming
charges with their supplier before
arriving in Hungary. Roaming charges
within the EU have been abolished
for member countries, but can be
very high for visitors from outside the
EU (so UK visitors need to check, too).

PHOTOGRAPHY

In some museums you have to pay a
fee in order to take photos or videos
(usually Ft500–2,000). &See also
Viewpoints p. 106.

POSTAL SERVICE

Letter boxes are usually red and
decorated with a hunting horn.
Stamps are sold in post offices. Post
cards take around 3–8 days to reach
the UK (1–2 weeks the US). Stamps to
send a postcard within Europe cost
Ft400 and Ft470 to the USA.
&See Business hours p. 97.

PUBLIC HOLIDAYS

103

- 1 January: New Year's Day
- 15 March: a national holiday
  (anniversary of the 1848–49
  Revolution)
- Easter: Good Friday to Easter
Monday
- Pentecost and Whit Monday
- 1 May: Labour Day
- 20 August: St. Stephen's Day/
  National Day
- 23 October: proclamation of the
  Republic of Hungary in 1989, and
  anniversary of the 1956 Hungarian
  Uprising
- 1 November: All Saints' Day
- 25 and 26 December: Christmas

PUBLIC TRANSPORT

Budapest
The capital has a very efficient and
practical transport system run by

BKK. See their site **bkk.hu/en** (in English) for timetables, information and downloads.

Buses, trams and trolleybuses generally operate 4.30am–11pm and the metro 4.30am–11.50pm (Fri & Sat until around 0.30am for lines M2 and M4). Night buses operate outside these hours. In Budapest there is also a riverbus service (6.30am–8.30pm, every 30/60min), plus a funicular to the castle *(p. 16)*. *See also Getting to Budapest p. 3.*

Around Lake Balaton

Although public transport is of course available, travelling by car is still the most practical way to discover the region in more depth ... or by bike perhaps, if you'd like to really earn those hearty Hungarian meals *(see p. 98)*.

Bus – *menetrendek.hu.* Numerous buses connect the different villages and towns around the lake. Fast and frequent, they often prove more convenient than the train to get from one locality to another.

Train – *mavcsoport.hu/en.* Two railway lines serve the lake – one running along the north shore to Tapolca, the other following the south shore to Keszthely. The two lines don't link up, but a bus connects Tapolca and Keszthely (a journey of around 1hr).

Ferry – *balatonihajozas.hu.* End June–beg Sept: every 40 min, 6.40am–11.20pm; check the website for times for rest of the year. Ft700/person, Ft400/bike, Ft1,900/car. The ferry operates between Tihany and Szántód all year round.

SMOKING/VAPING

Only tobacconists (marked with a green T) sell cigarettes in Hungary. Smoking and vaping are forbidden in public places: restaurants, cafés, pubs and on public transport and at the transport stops, but you can still smoke/vape on restaurant and café terraces.

TAXIS

There are plenty of taxis on the streets, their drivers either working independently or for a company. Ask about the price before you start and keep an eye on the meter, scams are not unknown. Watch out for unlicensed cabs – check the company logo is on the car door or on the light fixed to the roof and that it does not simply say 'Taxi'. To avoid the risk of picking an unlicensed cab, call one in advance. The following companies have a good reputation:

City Taxi – ☎ (1) 211 1111.
Főtaxi – ☎ (1) 222 2222.
Budapest Taxi – ☎ (1) 777 7777.
6X6 Taxi – ☎ (1) 666 6666.
See also Getting to Budapest p. 3.

THERMAL BATHS

If you have never been to Hungary before, a great treat awaits. More than 300 of the thermal springs that gush out of the ground have been put to use in baths and spa complexes right across the country. It is a long-established tradition, stretching back to Roman times. People go to enjoy the therapeutic benefits of

WOW HUNGARY

wowhungary.com

HUNGARY,
THE WELLSPRING
OF WONDERS

TIHANY

the waters or just to relax, or often both. Each baths complex has its own character and atmosphere: a hint of the Orient from the legacy of the Turkish occupation; the splendour of Art Nouveau or the Baroque; a more clinical environment suited to modern wellness treatments and therapies; or fun for families. And if you visit the thermal lake at Hévíz, your abiding memory will surely be floating in its warm waters among the waterlilies. ᕋSee p. 86.

TIPPING

A service charge is often not included in the bill (if it is included, you will see the words *szerviz díj* written on the menu or the bill). Otherwise, if you wish to leave a tip (at your discretion), 10–15% of the bill total is usual.

TOURIST PUBLICATIONS

Budapest's Finest, an English quarterly magazine published by the Budapest Festival and Tourism Centre and available in the Tourinform offices and in most hotels (it can also be downloaded at: budapestinfo.hu). It selects the best the city has to offer from among its places of interest, museums and cultural sites, shops, restaurants, and so on, and also lists events happening in the city.
Budapest Funzine – a monthly magazine in English (funzine.hu), also giving information on the latest events in the city, with good ideas for things to do.

Funzine also produces a **Lake Balaton special** twice a year (autumn and spring, in English and German), with plenty of suggestions and up-to-the-minute information (funzine.hu/en/category/balaton-en/). It is widely available in tourist offices, some shops, restaurants and hotels.

Newspapers
Most English-language newspapers are available in shops and on newsstands in Budapest and the major resorts on Lake Balaton.

VIEWPOINTS

You can take some fantastic photos in Budapest, even with the most ancient of phones or the most basic of cameras, the whole city is just so photogenic. But for advice on where to get some really great shots, particularly if yours is a flying visit, try these suggestions:
views over the Danube and the city, from the **Buda Castle district** (Buda side of the city, *p. 16*) and the **Danube Promenade** (Pest side, *p. 18*).
As for Lake Balaton, you could almost say that snapping a selfie with a luscious backdrop is de rigueur here. And there are a number of **observation towers** (*kilátó*) built on high points that make this super easy, designed with the sole purpose of opening your eyes to the fabulous views. The best are at: Balatonfüred (*p. 34*), Balatonalmádi (*p. 28*) and Balatonboglár (*p. 30*).
Many of the **wine terraces** around Badacsony also have superb views of the lake (*p. 78*).

WATER SPORTS

Catamaran Base – *Alsóörs (north shore). Füredi utca 1. ℰ (20) 984 8801. katamaran.hu.* As you will have guessed, this centre specializes in catamarans (lessons and chartering). They also offer mini discovery cruises of 1 hour if you don't want to take the rudder yourself.

SUPort – *Siófok (south shore). Aranypart, Móricz Zsigmond utca 20. ℰ (30) 476 8885. supshop.hu.* Standup paddleboarding has spread to the shores of Lake Balaton, as this centre demonstrates. They also offer yoga classes.

Tihany (north shore)

Sail & Surf – *Rév utca 3 (next to the Club Tihany hotel). ℰ (30) 22 789 27. www.wind99.com/en.* How about taking advantage of the shallow waters of the lake to (re)take up windsurfing or sailing (beginners and advanced). This yacht club is a local landmark, with instructors who speak English.

Aktív Pont Tihany – *Lepkesor 11. ℰ (30) 435 65 36. aktivponttihany.hu.* Hire a boat here, which can be anything from a dinghy upwards, for a trip either accompanied by an English-speaking skipper or skippering yourself. This centre offers a whole range of services linked to sailing and they also hire out bikes or can take you on a guided walk.

WINE TOURISM

Many visitors to the Lake Balaton area make the most of their stay by visiting a wine cellar or two – understandably so, since it is one of Hungary's 22 wine-growing regions. There has been quite a push in recent years towards developing wine tourism in hotels and restaurants, guest houses and places where you can sip a glass or two on a terrace overlooking the lake. Badacsony has been a focus for this activity on the north shore, but wineries and cellars in Balatonfüred, Tihany and Balatonboglár on the south shore are now also open to the public. And the creation of a Lake Balaton wine route is also underway. *(Open-air wine terraces, ⏱see pp. 76–79.)*

Hungarian Names

Hungary is unusual in being one of the few countries in which a person's full name is given in the Eastern order, as in Japan and China, where names are presented in the order of surname followed by the given name. That is why you will visit the Liszt Ferenc Emlékmúzeum in Budapest, rather than the Ferenc Liszt Emlékmúzeum. And some of the names of famous Hungarians with whom you are familiar are anglicized versions. Most visitors will know of Franz Liszt, but will be unfamiliar with his first name in Hungarian – Ferenc.

Festivals and events

ANNUAL EVENTS

April
▶**Spring Festival – Budapest**
Classical and contemporary music, jazz, theatre, operettas, opera, folk groups, Hungarian and foreign ballet companies, films at various venues across the city.
btf.hu/events

May–June
▶**Jewish Cultural Festival – Budapest**
Concerts, poetry, theatre in various venes across the city.
zsidomuveszetinapok.hu

June
▶**Danube Carnival – Budapest**
An international festival of dance and music (including classical, contemporary, folk, world).
dunakarneval.hu
▶**Night of the Museums – the whole country**
Around 20–25 June. Events held at and free entry to the museums, 6pm–1am. muzej.hu
  Szigliget Castle Festival
In mid-June and against a perfect backdrop, tournaments, chivalrous knights and falconry take the castle back to its medieval heyday over two days. szigligeti-var

July
▶**Open-air Film Festival – Budapest**
A film is shown in front of the Parliament Building every day 4.30pm–11pm.

▶**Valley of the Arts Festival – Kapolcs (Badacsony)**
 Held over 10 days in July. One of the oldest festivals in Hungary (from 1989), in and around Badacsony.
muveszetekvolgye.hu
▶**Anna Ball – Balatonfüred**
The Anna Grand Hotel on 26 July, a date and place in all the best diaries. A little like a debutantes' ball, the parade of guests in period costume is a spectacle in itself, reviving the spirit of the resort's golden age.
▶**Kékszalag (Blue Ribbon Regatta) – Balatonfüred**
Held at the beginning of July since 1934, the longest yacht race on a lake in Europe.

July–October
▶**Sparties – Budapest**. Sparties (pool parties) take over Széchenyi Baths on Saturday evenings *(p. 87)*.
bathsbudapest.com
▶**Balaton Sound – Zamárdi**
(5km/3mi east of Szántód)
For 5 days during July, one of the biggest open-air music festivals in Europe. balatonsound.com
▶**Vajdahunyad Summer music Festival – Budapest**
Concerts of klezmer (traditional Jewish music), Romani and classical music in the castle courtyard.
vajdahunyadcastle.com

August
▶**Jazzpiknik – Paloznak**
(6km/3.5mi east of Balatonfüred)
For three days at the beginning of

Balaton Sound, Zamárdi

August. Open-air jazz concerts, with cafés and bars. jazzpiknik.hu

▶**Sziget Festival – Budapest**
Lasting a week in mid-August. Young music fans flock to this Glastonbury-style music festival on Óbuda Island. szigetfestival.com

▶**Festival of Folk Arts – Budapest**
Held in the Buda Castle district. The festival reaches its climax with the 20 August celebrations, including fireworks.
www.mestersegekunnepe.hu

Lellei Borhét – Balatonlelle
(4km/2.5mi east of Balatonboglár) A week-long festival celebrating the wines of Lelle, with tastings and folk traditions galore.
balatonlelle.hu

September

▶**International Wine Festival – Budapest**
The second week of September. A fair, wine auction, grape harvest celebration and concerts on the forecourt of Buda Palace.
aborfesztival.hu

▶**Balaton Piknik – Balatonboglár**
Second weekend in September. Rock and electro concerts at the Gömbkilátó observatory, transformed into a stage. www.balatonpiknik.hu

▶**European Heritage Days – the whole country**
During the third weekend in September. Many places that are usually closed to the public are opened up, with some also offering lectures and concerts.

October

▶**Café Budapest Contemporary Arts Festival – Budapest**
Contemporary and experimental art (films, music, displays).
cafebudapestfest.hu

November

▶**Füred Gastro – Balatonfüred**
The clue is in the name – a food festival held during the second weekend in November.
gastrofured.hu

December

▶**Gypsy Symphony Orchestra – Budapest**
A Gala concert on 30 December.

▶**Christmas market – Budapest**
In the city centre.

▶**Gala and Opera Ball – Budapest**
The great New Year's Eve celebration on 31 December.

Find out more

Tins of paprika
© E. Fleisher/Look/Photononstop

Key dates

1–4C AD – The **Romans** found the province of Pannonia (in the west of present-day Hungary). Aquincum (the future Budapest) becomes a flourishing city.

5C AD – The **Huns** capture Aquincum.

896 – The **Magyars** cross the Carpathian Mountains. Prince Árpád sets up his summer camp on Csepel Island in the Danube.

1055 – King András (Andrew) I founds the Benedictine Abbey in **Tihany**.

1182 – Monks from Clairvaux in France found **Zirc Abbey** at the request of King Béla III.

1241 – Buda and Pest are devastated by the **Tartar** invasion.

1243 – King Béla IV builds **Buda Castle**.

1260 – **Szigliget Castle** is built on the northern shore of Lake Balaton.

1458–90 – Under the reign of **Matthias Corvinus** (Matthias I), Buda becomes one of Europe's cultural centres.

1541 – The **Turks** conquer Buda.

1601 – Fire destroys Székesfehérvár Basilica where the kings of Hungary had been crowned and many are buried.

1686 – The Christian armies led by Habsburg prince **Charles V, duke of Lorraine**, liberate the city. Buda becomes a garrison town for the Austrian army.

1739 – **Count Kristóf Festetics** builds Keszthely Castle.

1795 – The first bathing pavilions appear at **Hévíz** thermal lake.

1825 – Count István Széchenyi builds the Chain Bridge in Budapest; the first Anna Ball is held in Balatonfüred.

1846 – The first steamboat is launched on Lake Balaton.

1848–49 – The **Hungarian Revolution** against the Habsburgs.

1861 – A railway is constructed along the southern shore of Lake Balaton.

1867 – The Austro-Hungarian compromise and creation of the Dual Monarchy: **Emperor Franz Joseph** of Austria and his wife Elisabeth are crowned sovereigns of Hungary.

1873 – The **unification** of Buda, Pest and Óbuda as one city: Budapest.

1878 – Balatonfüred opens its first medicinal water treatment room.

1896 – The first **metro line** (now the M1) in continental Europe opens in Budapest. Millennial celebrations for the Magyar conquest.

1902 – The inauguration of the Hungarian **Parliament building**.

1909 – The construction of a railway line on the northern shore of the lake.

1913 – The State Hospital for Cardiology opens in Balatonfüred.

1920 – The **Treaty of Trianon** redefines the Hungarian borders, after separation from Austria in 1918.

1934 – The first Kékszalag (Blue Ribbon) regatta is held on Lake Balaton, making it the oldest round-the-lake competition in Europe.

1944 – A reign of terror by the Arrow Cross Party, allies of the Nazis.

1945 – The Russian Red Army frees the city at the end of World War II.

Szigliget Castle on Lake Balaton's north shore

1949 – Communist minister **László Rajk** is tried and executed.

23 October–November 1956 – A **popular uprising**. In November Imre Nagy (prime minister) returns to power and announces neutrality and withdrawal from the Warsaw Pact. Soviet tanks enter the city and crush the uprising; an estimated 3,000 are killed. The city is devastated; 200,000 Hungarians leave the country.

1962 – The discovery of the thermal spring at Zalakaros (in the Lake Balaton region).

1989 – Imre Nagy (executed in 1958) is rehabilitated and reburied with full honours. On 23 October the People's Republic of Hungary becomes the **Republic of Hungary**. Red stars disappear from public buildings.

1991 – The last of the Russian troops leave Budapest.

1992 – Nationalized in 1948, Herend porcelain factory (opened in 1825) is bought back by its employees.

1996 – Bavaria returns the arm bone relic of St. Gisela, first queen of Hungary, to Veszprém

2004 – Hungary joins the **European Union**.

From 2010 – The Hungarian political landscape changes: Fidesz, the right-wing party led by prime minister **Viktor Orbán**, wins a majority and is re-elected in 2014 and 2018.

2023 – Veszprém is European Capital of Culture for a year.

The 'Hungarian Sea'

HISTORY

'Balaton' derives from the Avar word *blatno*, meaning 'stagnant water', in reference to its marshy areas, which are still present today, particularly around Tihany. The lake is an abundant source of life, supporting many kinds of freshwater fish, game and reedbeds.

Lake Balaton has long drawn people to its shores in search of quiet contemplation, attracted by its location and the particular quality of light, as the Benedictine monks who settled in Tihany in the 11C would have found. In the 16C the lake formed a kind of natural border, separating the Habsburgs from the Turks.

In the 18C the Germans, Croats and Slovaks began to settle and build in the region and by the end of this same century, Balatonfüred and Hévíz had started to take shape as holiday resorts. Wealthy families from Buda, Pest and Austria would come to spend their summers by the lake. The **railway linking Nagykanizsa and Buda** was built on the southern shore in 1861, while the northern shore rail link was installed in 1909. It was at this time that the lake, part of which had been backfilled, took on its current shape and that tourism began to develop on a large scale. It grew so much that in the period after the First World War, between 50,000 to 60,000 people were taking their annual holidays in Lake Balaton. Just 20 years later, on the eve of the Second World War, that figure had risen to around a quarter of a million.

A COMMUNIST RIVIERA

The socialist regime that became established in Hungary after the Second World War wanted to develop a form of social tourism that would benefit the workers. This led to the **nationalization** of existing facilities, the expropriation of villas and the construction of holiday centres. Alongside those opened by companies or workers' organizations, others, such as Balatonaliga holiday resort, were reserved for party members. The hierarchy was still

Sprechen Sie Deutsch ?

The use of German remains widespread around Lake Balaton. It is an unexpected legacy of the Communist period and when Germany was divided into East and West. Since both East and West Germans were allowed to enter Hungary on a visa and the drive from Germany was easy, in the 1960s and 70s many German families living on different sides of the border would reunite at the lake for their holidays. The generation that served them in commercial establishments is still in business, which is why you still hear German spoken in shops, restaurants and hotels.

© Reinhard Kaufhold/ZB/DPA/Photononstop

Lake Balaton in the 1970s

115

respected within this protected environment, with the amount of space allocated to holidaymakers and the quality of service and facilities available dependent on the status of the individual concerned. It was during this era that large social housing buildings were constructed, which in the 1990s were transformed into hotels. Some of these buildings, such as **Ezüstpart Hotel** in Siófok, are now regarded as architectural gems that typified their era, and are gradually being maintained and valued as such.

AND TODAY...

Today the Balaton region continues to play a key role in Hungary's tourism industry. After Budapest, it is the most visited area of the country, and each year **1.8 million tourists** spend time in the different resorts on its shores or in the hinterland. On long weekends during the high season, the Budapest locals swell the ranks of German tourists, who make up the largest number of visitors (↻*see panel p. 114*).

The lake's success is due to its lovely natural surroundings, its microclimate and the facilities on offer, all of which contribute to making the area so popular. Holidaymakers wanting to rest and relax or play sport and enjoy water-based activities can choose from some 130 beaches and a wide range of facilities on offer and at different prices.

Thermal baths

A SOCIAL MILIEU

Just where are people going in the early morning or evening, clutching a small waterproof bag? The chances are they are heading off to the baths (open from 6am), equipped with toiletries and other personal effects. The baths are a reminder of the Roman era and the Ottoman occupation and have long been part of life in Hungary. Whether in Budapest, Balatonfüred or Székesfehérvár, Hungarians visit them to soothe aches and pains, chat, play chess and relax.

A SENSE OF WELLBEING

A visit to the baths normally produces a genuine sense of wellbeing. Spa-goers might finish a session with a steam bath, massage and, of course, a shower. The effect is a kind of 'decompression' and release, and sometimes a sharpening of the appetite. It would be a real shame to leave Hungary without taking the chance to visit one of these places, even if it is only to admire the wonderful buildings in which some of them are housed.

© Ikonya/iStock

Hévíz thermal lake

ETIQUETTE

You will need to pay attention to the day on which you decide to visit the baths since they offer mixed bathing and separate times for men and women. Note that during single-sex bathing periods, many people will not be wearing costumes. You will need a bathing costume, towel and waterproof sandals (they can also be hired at some of the baths). A swimming cap is generally required for swimming pools (you can often buy one if you haven't come equipped) and a waterproof bag is useful for carrying your belongings to and from the different baths (shampoo, soap and brush...). Hairdryers are usually available. Once inside, there will be a choice of different pools, varying from thermal pools, those for activities and others that are just for swimming. You will often find Turkish baths (hammams), steam rooms and saunas, too. And if you start to feel peckish, most baths have somewhere that you can buy snacks and drinks.

AN ANCIENT RITUAL

Budapest and the surrounding areas are awash with hot springs. There are over a hundred, some of which supply the thermal spa complexes of the capital. Their therapeutic powers did not escape the attention of the Romans, who had already acquired the bathing habit back home and used them extensively, as can be seen from the ruins of the ancient thermal baths at Aquincum.

In the 16C the Ottoman Turks, who occupied Hungary for over a century and a half, developed the public baths further and built some of the architectural gems that are still carefully maintained and used today. The current trend is for large spa complexes, with one section reserved for therapeutic treatments and another for more family-friendly, recreational activities.

It would of course be impossible to list all the spas in Budapest and the Lake Balaton region. We have included the best-known and those that are of the most interest from the architectural point of view and hence are worth seeing in their own right. Many of the spa buildings are simply beautiful, ranging from Turkish domes over atmospherically lit octagonal pools to statues, sculptures and the elaborate ornamentation of the neo-Baroque and Secessionist styles. (⌖ See p. 86).

Goulash and paprika

Rich in flavour and spice and yet mellow on the palate, Hungarian cuisine echoes the long journey taken by the Magyars from Asia. Their nomadic traditions enjoyed a culinary cross-fertilization, mixing with those of the Turks, Bavarians and Bulgarians, while the Austro-Hungarian influence culminated in the art of patisserie.

The Lake Balaton region has recently undergone a gastronomic resurgence, with restaurants offering dishes full of flavour based on local ingredients and accompanied by some excellent regional wines.

TYPICAL DISHES

Ingredients – The local cuisine makes regular use of a roux, to which is added a generous quantity of onions to form the base of a sauce that is then made very piquant with red **paprika**, the ubiquitous spice that lends its name (*paprikás*) to many of the dishes that are made with it, in particular fish, poultry and veal.

Starters – The Turks introduced the *pogácsa,* small, crispy, salted scones made with wheat flour or potato and containing lard, and cheese or spices.

Main dishes: soup – A staple feature of Hungarian cuisine, including *Jókai bableves*, a bean soup garnished with strips of smoked pork and sausage. *Hortobágyi húsos palacsinta* is a thick savoury pancake, folded over and filled with meat and onions.

Soup and meat – The most famous Hungarian dish has to be *gulyás*, a beef soup made with onions and paprika, and sometimes potatoes or carrots. Goulash, as it is generally understood outside Hungary, is called *pörkölt* within it: a stew made with braised meat, tomatoes and green peppers, with a pronounced flavour of onion. Roasted pork shank (*csülök*) is equally popular and features on the menu of many small restaurants.

It may come as a surprise to learn that foie gras (*libamáj*) also graces the Hungarian table across the seasons. It is served as an escalope or in large cubes fried in goose fat and served with a little garlic and onion.

There is a wide array of sausages, in particular top-notch salami.

Vegetables – Dishes are often served with rice, homemade pasta that resembles gnocchi and is known as *galuska*, or a mix of flour and eggs rolled into small balls and fried gently in lard (*tarhonya*). Green vegetables do not feature much except in top restaurants. Salad, when it does appear, usually comprises cucumber, pickled cabbage or peppers in vinegar.

Fish – The most common fish is pike-perch or *fogas*. Catfish is also popular, freshly caught in Lake Balaton. Carp (*ponty*) is served in breadcrumbs or 'Serbian' style with a sprinkling of paprika. *Halászlé* is a soup made only with freshwater fish, including carp, catfish and pike, to which paprika is often added. In some restaurants, particularly during the summer, it is made outside in huge cauldrons over an open fire and can be highly spiced.

Lángos – Garnished with sour cream and cheese, this deep-fried flatbread is a favourite snack around the lake. It also represents the perfect Hungarian street food; its great flavour is taken to new levels when accompanied by a *fröccs*, a sparkling wine and soda spritzer using Olaszrizling, the favourite wine of Balaton locals.

DESSERTS AND SWEETS

Crêpes – *Palacsinta* are served with a huge array of fillings, which include sweetened cottage cheese, nuts or apricot jam.

Cakes – Pastries made with poppy seeds, apples or nuts are traditional in Central Europe. The cottage cheese turnover (*túrós batyu*) can look very modest next to a piece of *Dobos torta*, invented by the famous pastry chef József Dobos, comprising seven layers of Genoese sponge with rich chocolate buttercream, cut into slices, each of which is topped with a triangle of sponge coated in orange caramel. *Rigó Jancsi* is a chocolate sponge cake with a whipped chocolate cream filling. Few can resist *somlói galuska*, a melt-in-the-mouth sponge cake-based dessert, flavoured with rum and filled with nuts and raisins. It is served with whipped cream. *Rétes* is a type of strudel made with layers of puff pastry and filled with apples, cottage cheese, poppy

seeds, nuts or sour cherries. The very popular *túró rudi* is a chocolate bar filled with cream cheese. *Kürtőskalács* is a 'chimney cake' baked on a spit over an open fire and served plain or with a sprinkling of sugar or chocolate.

WINE AND ALCOHOL

Wines from the Balaton region – The valleys around Lake Balaton are home to a number of microclimates and to some of the best Hungarian vineyards. To the north, the volcanic soils of Badacsony and Somló deliver well-structured white wines. Somló wines are made using local grape varieties that include Juhfark, Furmint and Hárslevelű. Badacsony and Balatonfüred produce delicious Pinot Gris (known in Hungary as Szürkebarát), Olaszrizling and Kéknyelű, an unusual wine unique to the region.

Beer – On tap or bottled, beer (*sör*) is widely available, with local brands including Dréher, Soproni and Borsodi.

Pálinka – Hungarians rarely drink wine at lunchtime but schnapps is very popular. Prepare to be offered some of their famous *pálinka* as a digestif.

119

Index

Maps

Inside
Tihany Peninsula *p41*

Cover
Budapest and Lake Balaton
  Inside front cover

Detachable map
Budapest *Front*
Lake Balaton *Back*

Photo credits

Page 4
Szent-György Hill: © Patrick Frilet/hemis.fr
Veszprém: © Tibor Bognár/age fotostock
Parliament Building: © Jon Arnold Images/hemis.fr
Hévíz thermal lake: © Bertrand Gardel/hemis.fr
Székesfehérvár: © Hungarian Tourism Agency

Page 5
North Shore: © Reinhard Schmid/Sime/Photononstop
Keszthely: © csakisti/iStock
Tihany: © I love takeing photos and i think that is a really great opportunity for me to share them/iStock
Thermal baths: © ProjectB/iStock
Buda Castle and Castle District: © emicristea/iStock

Symbols in the guide

★★★ **Worth a special journey**   ★★ **Worth a detour**   ★ **Interesting**

Hotels and Restaurants

9 rms	Number of rooms
bc	Beverage menu included
cc	Payment by credit card
	Credit cards not accepted
	Air conditioning in room
✕	Restaurant in hotel
♀	Alcohol served
	Swimming pool

Symbols

	Also see
♿	Disabled Access
	A bit of advice / consider
	Recommended
A2 B	Map coordinates

Maps and Plans

MONUMENTS AND SITES

	Catholic Church
	Protestant church - other temple
	Synagogue
	Mosque
	Calvary, wayside cross - Fountain
	Rampart - Tower - Gate
Ⅶ	Viewpoint
	Observation area
∩	Quarry

INFORMATION

	Tourist information
	Parking - Park-and-Ride
	Tramway - Underground - Métro
	Train station - Coach (bus) station
	Cable cars
	Funicular - rack railway
	Tourist train
	Post office - Covered market
	Ferry service: cars and passengers
	Passengers only

ADDITIONAL SYMBOLS

	Motorway - Other primary route
	Pedestrian street
	Unsuitable for traffic - restrictions
	Escalator
	Footpath
B F	Car - Ferry
	Drawbridge

SPORTS AND RECREATION

	Swimming: open air - covered
	Stadium
	Racecourse
	Marina - Sailing center

ABBREVIATIONS

H	Town Hall	P	Local authority offices
J	Law courts	POL.	Police station
M	Museum	T	Theatre

THE GREEN GUIDE short-stays **Lake Balaton**

Editorial Director	Cynthia Ochterbeck
Editor	Sophie Friedman
Translator/Editor	JMS Books LLP
Production Manager	Natasha George
Cartography	Peter Wrenn, Nicolas Breton, Géraldine Deplante
Picture Editor	Yoshimi Kanazawa
Interior Design	Laurent Muller
Layout	Natasha George

Contact Us

Michelin Travel and Lifestyle North America
One Parkway South
Greenville, SC 29615
USA
travel.lifestyle@us.michelin.com

Michelin Travel Partner
Hannay House
39 Clarendon Road
Watford, Herts WD17 1JA
UK
℘01923 205240
travelpubsales@uk.michelin.com
www.viamichelin.co.uk

Special Sales

For information regarding bulk sales,
customized editions and premium sales,
please contact us at:
travel.lifestyle@us.michelin.com